To Gary

— Enjoy

Alux

5. 3. 12.

The WiZard Book of Management

An essential modern manager's toolkit containing 100 top tips

Arnie Skelton & Diane Ingham-Cook

authorHOUSE®

AuthorHouse™ UK Ltd.
500 Avebury Boulevard
Central Milton Keynes, MK9 2BE
www.authorhouse.co.uk
Phone: 08001974150

First published by AuthorHouse 12/01/2011

ISBN: 978-1-4520-9026-9 (sc)

Any people depicted in stock imagery provided by Thinkstock are models,
and such images are being used for illustrative purposes only.
Certain stock imagery © Thinkstock.

This book is printed on acid-free paper.

Introduction – What's in it for you?

This book has been written for those just moving into management; for those who have had little or no management development; for aspiring managers; and for those established managers wanting fresh ideas. So if you fit the bill—this is for you!

A book that's different from all the others on the market. We have set out to make it practical, and jargon free. It's based on our own ideas, as a manager, management trainers and company directors. The aim is to provide some new perspectives on familiar problems, and offer 100 solutions, ideas and tools that many managers have told us, have made a real difference.

Some tips contain a single but important idea: others tackle a typical difficulty, and offer a range of suggestions. You can read the book from front to back, or may be better still, dip and collect a tip as required, take what's relevant for you and try it.

Thanks for showing an interest in this book, it will provide you with some '**magic**' answers that help and encourage you. Enjoy!

Being Professional
a useful starting point....
Imagine you own your own company (maybe you do) what do you expect of your managers?

We imagine your standards are very high!

All managers, are responsible for their side of the deal; there are legitimate expectations others have of those in a management role. Others would include, your team, your boss, your peer group and those outside but integral to your organisation and its reputation. Great managers also have high expectations of themselves, and work to ensure others can deliver excellent performance.

If you are a manager, of course you'll know there are many challenges and no guarantee of results, but your job is to be professional , and do your best every day.

Being professional ..

...doing a job you don't like with someone you don't like and it doesn't show at all !

Where to find what you want?

For easy use we've identified 6 sections that contain what a modern manager does.

It begins with you   ... all about managing yourself

Getting it right with others   ...importance of managing relationships

Getting results   ...about managing performance

Finding the way forward   ...can help with managing problems & decision making

Working with what you have   ...tips on managing resources

In the know   ... hints on managing context & change

To let you know …

The above guide will help to give the book structure and shape, although many of the hints and tips could have appeared in several sections. For example; some of the ideas for **getting it right with others** could equally apply to it **starts with you** …and vice versa.

The Magic!   It Starts With You

Contents

1
ASSERTIVENESS:
-Making a difficult request

It can feel uncomfortable to make a difficult request so why not try the 'when...I...so...' technique:

> "**when** you...(name the behaviour)

> "**I**... (describe your uncomfortable response, and the consequence of this)

> "**So**... (suggest a preferred alternative)

For example:

"when you often agree to my request for a meeting, and then cancel at short notice, I feel you regard the meeting as unimportant or low priority, so I feel my work and requests are devalued. So I'd prefer it if you could keep to our arrangement '.

Naturally you should choose your own form of words, according to the relationship you have with that person, and how comfortable you feel saying it—but the three step principle is the same:

It may help in advance to

- identify the behaviour you struggle with
- explain the effect that behaviour has on you
- ask for a change that would work better for you

2
ASSERTIVENESS:
Tackle your fears

Break down your fears and anxiety into bite size chunks, then tackle them by prevention and coping strategies. This builds confidence, and reduces the likelihood of avoidance of the issue....

PROBLEM: (identify the main problem)

SPECIFIC	PREVENTION	COPING
What is the specific concern, worry or fear within the problem (may be several)	What can you do to prevent or minimise the chance of each of these concerns happening?	What's the best you can do if, despite your best efforts, it doesn't happen as planned?

3
ASSERTIVENESS:
Simply Saying No

The **ASS** technique

One consistent question from participants on our programmes is how can I say no?

Simply ...

A   Acknowledge the other person's request

S   Say no—and offer a reason if appropriate

S   Suggest the next best alternative

Example: your own manager asks you to stay late.

"I can see that it's important " (A)

"I've promised to take the kids swimming, so I can't stay late tonight" (S)

"but I'm happy to start on it first thing in the morning" (S)

Note: only give a reason for saying no if it's honest, and it feels discourteous not to

4
ASSERTIVENESS:
Saying no by saying yes

If your manager has a request for you, which is legitimate, you can't and shouldn't really say no.

So say "yes, of course"......

But follow it with:

> "this is what I have on at the moment, what would you like me to stop working on to make space for it?"

This emphasises that you are already fully occupied, and protects you from being driven into an ever expanding workload.

It converts the issue of saying no (negative) into one of prioritising (positive). If the new request is a priority, then that's fair enough—but something needs to come out of the workload in order to make space for this incoming work.

Your manager now has three legitimate options: to decide what you should stop working on; to confirm your current workload is a priority, and take the incoming work elsewhere; or ask you to 'do your best' - which leaves it up to you.

What is unreasonable is for the manager to insist you maintain your current workload and find the time/space for the new task. In this situation, you need to hold your ground, and try the 'holding the line' technique.

5
ASSERTIVENESS:
Holding the line

Sometimes you just have to stick to your guns, and 'hold the line'.

In such times, it's really important to choose your sticking point, then stick to it, whatever the other person says.

These three steps will help you do this:

1. choose your 'sticking point' (and know why it's important)
2. choose a phrase you feel comfortable saying, that makes your sticking point clear
3. acknowledge and accept the other person's points/ attempts to deflect you, but always repeat your sticking point.

Example: Refusal to take on new work when you already have a full workload

- "I can't take on more work without some other part of my workload being reduced"
- I accept that this is an emergency, however I cannot take on more work without some other part of my workload being reduced"

If you don't hold the line, then you may be bullied or browbeaten into conceding something which you cannot deliver, or which makes you uncomfortable and resentful later.

6
AVOIDANCE:
The gain-pain relationship

When faced with difficult situations, always consider which type of pain/gain relationship you want....

Which do you choose, in any difficult situation?

STG, LTP   or STP, LTG?

Sometimes it seems easier to concede in the short term, and pay the consequences in the longer term (short term gain, long term pain: STG LTP).

This is often the case, for example, if you are not sufficiently assertive. You may say 'yes' to please someone, or take the heat off, in the short term, but you will have to pay the consequences (doing the extra task, waiting to give someone the lift home) in the longer term.

Conversely, it may be worth considering the reverse relationship: short term pain, long term gain (STP , LTG). For example, saying no might be uncomfortable in the short term, but you may well get the long term benefit as a result.

Whatever you choose, make it a conscious one!

7
BEING POSITIVE:
It's your choice

We can all choose our attitude. It may take time and effort, but ultimately, how we feel belongs to us. If we don't choose how we feel—who does? And are you happy with that?

How we behave is heavily determined by our mood and attitude. So having a positive attitude and frame of mind will help us 'be' more positive in our behaviours and relationships.

Don't let your mood or attitude be determined by others, or circumstance: choose it for yourself.

Here are some ideas to help you:

- Take pleasure in doing the little things, all within your control, that please and help others
- Look to identify the positives in any situation, rather than the negatives (and that goes for people, too)
- Challenge any negative thinking that goes on in your head (your internal dialogue, or inner voice); if it is negative or restrictive, make sure you hear a counter-view, too
- Surround yourself with positives—things that you enjoy, that give your mood a lift
- Keep a sense of perspective; there are almost certainly others far worse off than you
- Moods are infectious; certainly it's easy to catch a negative mood from others: but what mood do others catch from you? Are you generally a positive or negative influence on others....?

8
BLIND SPOTS:
What do others see in you?

A blind spot is a behaviour you may have that has an impact on others, but which you are unaware of. The blind spot can be positive or negative.

There are two types of lack of awareness:

- You have no idea you are doing it
- You know you are doing it, but are unaware of its impact

Sadly people tend to focus on negative blind spots, but that's a pity—many of us have positive blind spots—ie characteristics and behaviours others appreciate and value, but which remain blind spots. If you think this might be the case for someone you manage or work with, give them the positive feedback. It will not only make them feel good, it is the best guarantee you have that they will continue to do it (now they know about it, and that it's appreciated).

Negative blind spots are of course, harder to address—it is likely to be an uncomfortable conversation. However, by its very nature, a blind spot cannot be corrected by the individual without them being made aware of it. How would you feel if you had a negative behaviour that you were completely unaware of? Would you want to know?

If you don't give blind spot feedback, then you have to take some responsibility for the continuation of that behaviour. Not to tackle it is to condone it.

If you have a positive working relationship with someone, then they are likely to take the feedback constructively—knowing the <u>intent</u> was to help, rather than to damage.

Generally speaking, offering blind spot feedback can be a gift.

Unless the individual knows, they can do nothing about it; blind spot feedback gives them the opportunity to move forward.

If you are concerned that you might have some negative blind spots, what can you do about this?

- Ask others in your team, or who are close to you, to give you blind spot feedback
- Learn to watch carefully for people's reactions to what you are saying and doing.

"The meaning of the communication is in the response you get"

In other words, other people's responses tell you a lot about how you are coming across.

9
FINDING THE BALANCE –
Check Yours

As a manager, there are several sets of balances you will have to find. Here are the most common:

1 Work	v	Home
2 Manager role	v	Specialist role
3 Quality	v	Quantity
4 Creating stability	v	Continuous development
5 Looking ahead	v	Dealing with current issues
6 Supporting your manager	v	Supporting your team
7 Meeting your needs	v	Meeting the needs of others

There may be others more relevant to you than these.

The point is this:

it is all about balance

Some you should discuss with others most affected:

The first on the list should involve your family. 2 to 6 you should discuss with your manager

Number 7 should be in your mind at all times. It's human instinct to put our own needs first. For example, suppose you wanted to have a meeting with one of your team. Who would decide where, when, and how—and why? As manager, you always need to consider the other person or group's needs, wants and preferences—put yourself in their shoes.

10
INTERNAL/EXTERNAL SELF:

Ever felt like you wanted to blow your top, but didn't because you thought it wouldn't help? Well that's because you consist of 2 different selves—the internal and external self.

The **external self** is the part of you that's visible, and impacts and creates an impression on others. The 3 ways externally of creating an impression are through how you **look, sound** and **act**.   Summarised as your behaviours.

Your **internal self** consists of how you **feel, think** and **believe**—these can be summarised as your attitude..

INTERNAL/EXTERNAL SELF

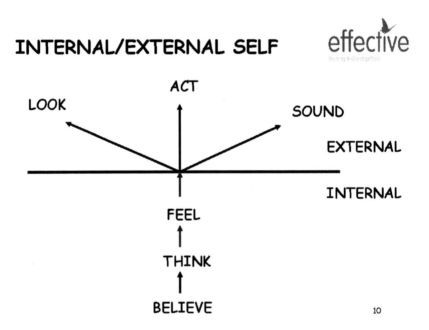

So it's good to know that..

- Our external self is heavily influenced by our internal self—but they can be separated, that's why you didn't 'blow your top'
- It's possible to behave well even if our internal self is negative—but it is hard work and stressful
- For the best long term results it is worth investing in being positive
- Many people go through life not knowing about their internal self, or not knowing that they can change it.
- Understanding this model can help you work with others who seem persistently negative- ie it may be worth tackling their negative internal self by discussing their external behaviour, and their reasons for it

11
TACKLING FEAR:
About face!

Fear is a repellent. As soon as we become aware of what we fear, we turn and move away from it. We literally do not face our fears—we always have our back to what we fear.

As a result, we rarely look at what we fear (face up to it) - so we rarely have a constructive strategy for what we fear. In order to tackle it, rather than continue to avoid it, we need to look at it carefully, to find out what it is, precisely, that we fear.

Fear is :

Fantasy
Expressed or Experienced
As
Reality

It is the fear of something, rather than the 'something' itself, that often holds us in check. So check for yourself

Is the 'fear' actually valid or not. ?

What if what we feared was actually a myth, or a sham?

How would we ever know, if the 'fear' itself prevents us from finding out?

What if you 'feared' public speaking, yet find out that when happens you actually really enjoy it and are good at it..? It's reasonable to weigh the costs or risks of doing something: that is rational. But fear is often irrational, and may prevent you getting huge benefits from life.

12
PERSONAL BRANDING:
One IDEA to define you

As a manager getting a positive response, acceptance and being able to influence those you work with is often affected by what people think about you.

So if you regard yourself as a 'product' - what are the things that create an image or a personal brand?

IDEA
I	identifier(s)
+	
D	discriminators
+	
E	emotional charge
=	
A	acceptance

The **identifier** gives the identity to the product or service;

For you this could be your name, title, job role etc

Discriminators are qualities that help separate a product from the rest of its competitors; what are your exceptional qualities? Reliability, sense of humour, depth of knowledge?

An **Emotional** charge is the impact or appeal a product has on the customer's heart and mind and for you as a manager what you do in specific areas which help create positive 'emotional' responses from others e.g. ability to listen and understand

Together these will help create brand/personal identity, acceptance and positive response from those who work with you.

13
POSITIVE INTERVENTION:
A modern manager

A modern view of management is 'positive intervention'.

It's based on an empowering view of work, ie one where staff have both the ability and will to manage themselves most of the time. This then means the manager's main two roles are to provide clear direction (including priorities), and the resources to ensure they can be met. The manager then only needs a 'light touch' to ensure all is well, and to provide regular and supportive feedback.

Most serious interventions, under this approach, are therefore to do with problems or difficulties—ie the occasion when the empowering model does not work. In such interventions, the manager needs to be positive at all times. 'Positive' here has two meanings:

- The manager's behaviours must always be positive— no matter how frustrating or difficult the challenge. The manager must be a positive role model, whatever the difficulty

- The manager's strategy must also be positive and constructive and mustn't abandon anyone they manage, no matter how tempting it sometimes can be!! The manager must provide positive and equal opportunity to all staff, at all times. There must be no sense of 'leaving them to get on with it'; of 'washing your hands' of a situation or person. Always assume that the breakthrough is possible, and, that if it doesn't occur, it won't be for lack of effort.

14
RESPONSE MANAGEMENT:
Donkey buttons

Remember the small wooden toys that sat on a little plinth with a button underneath , usually an animal like a donkey that collapsed when you pressed the button and when released the donkey would become upright again?

We are like that donkey. Mainly in control: upright, self assured and self confident most of the time, until something (or someone) comes along and pushes our donkey button. The button represents the the things that frustrate, annoy, confuse or create fear in us.

This can be accidental, or deliberate, but the effect is the same—we can become, weak, embarrassed, distracted, uncomfortable, afraid, annoyed..Things that can push our buttons can be big or small, for example the dishwasher not being stacked properly, or a member of the team taking long breaks. Our response once the button has been pushed could be anything from sulking to emotional outbursts…. and when that happens, know your button has been pushed!

So whoever has control over our donkey buttons, has control over us.The good news is, that we all own our own donkey buttons and we allow them to be pushed. And what we allow, we can prevent. So—work out what and where your donkey buttons are—then turn them off. If you don't manage your donkey buttons—who does??

Saying it, of course, is much easier than doing it. But the first step is to recognise that you have such buttons, and identify how to control them, rather than the people who push them.

15
RESPONSE MANAGEMENT:
Choose Your Own Response

Being responsible is all about choosing your response.

P + R = O   P : provocation   R :response O : outcome

Provocation consists of all those things that impact on us that we would rather didn't – from getting stuck in a traffic jam to losing our job. Provocations are inevitable; they are external to us, we have no choice over them, no control over them happening...live life, you'll be provoked.

Response consists of what you do with those provocations. Your response is internal to you, something you have choice over, and (if you choose), control.

The same provocation will produce different responses from different people. So

- Whatever the provocation
- You own the response
- The difference is in the response
- The difference is in you

It is the provocation, plus the way you respond to it, that will determine the **outcome** you get. The same provocation will produce different outcomes in people, because they chose different responses. For example shouting as a response will produce a different outcome from talking calmly.

Responsibility is response—**ability**.

16
RESPONSIBILITY:
Stop Worrying!

The 3, 2, 1 technique - We've been told this is a life saver.

Create a list of everything—everything—that's a concern to you.

Don't cheat, make sure you do your list before reading on!

Then score each item on the list a 3, 2 or 1, according to the following:

- 3: beyond my control or influence to do anything about this
- 2: beyond my control, but I may be able to influence ie I can't control it, but I can try and influence those who do
- 1: within my control (ie down to me)

OK, now for each score there is a strategy:

- 3: Everything you scored a 3 - Let it go (including no worrying or blaming)
- 2: Nothing should stay scored a 2. It's decision time, so do a quick cost-benefit analysis: if the benefits of trying to influence outweigh the costs involved, move it to a 1; if they don't—move it to a 3.
- 1: For scores of 1 do it—or prioritise it. (Key point for all 1s: if you don't do it, it won't get done)

You should now be clear about what you can and can't do and will enable you to stop worrying or grumbling (how does that help?). Do what you can, and let the rest go....

17
RESPONSIBILITY:
Being Professional

Alignment

We are two people at work. We are individuals, with likes, dislikes, hopes, fears, expectations, preferences….this is our personal self. We are also at work in our formal roles, and the organisation and its workforce has expectations of us in this formal role. This is our professional self. Alignment refers to the extent to which our personal and professional selves are in harmony, or aligned.

Most of the time, hopefully, they will be. But from time to time, what you might want and prefer as an individual isn't what the organisation wants from you in your formal role. Similarly, the organisation might want you to carry out tasks that, personally, you don't like.

In any clash between the personal and professional self, the professional self must win every time.

For it to be otherwise, there would be no organisation— everyone could do as they pleased. If you disagree with a policy, you can challenge it—but so long as it is legitimate, you should carry it out—and to the best of your ability. This can be crucial for example, when asked to introduce an unpopular change. A good definition of

'professionalism' is doing a task you don't like, with someone you don't like, to the best of your ability. If anyone is unaligned most of the time, they are probably in the wrong job….

18
RESPONSIBILITY:
Customer Satisfaction!

R = LEO
R: Responsibility   L: Legitimate   E: Expectations of
O: Others

Simply, your responsibilities are equivalent to the legitimate expectations that others have of you in your role.

This is a **customer-centred** model, in that your role is defined by your customer expectations. Identify all those who you work with, and think what their expectations are of you in that role. If they are legitimate, then they should become your responsibility. (Best of all, talk to them about this).

In your role as manager, who crucially do you work with in this role? Your staff, your own manager, colleagues and others outside the organisation. Talk to them. Find out their expectations and preferences. If they seem legitimate, then they need to become your responsibility.

This technique is also useful for getting you to see your staff as customers of your management service. What do they expect from you as their manager? Are these expectations legitimate? If they are, they need to become your responsibility—otherwise you will produce customer dissatisfaction....

19
SELF-CONFIDENCE:
The Confidence Triangle

3 things affect our level of confidence

FEAR

SELF IMAGE   SELF CONTROL

Fear: fear acts as a repellent; we tend to move away from fear, so we rarely, if ever, face it. So if confronted with our fears, we have no strategy thought through in advance for dealing with it.

(See Tip 11 on fear)

Self image: how you see and think of yourself. Many of us have a lower opinion of ourselves than our colleagues do; we dwell on, and exaggerate, our apparent flaws and weaknesses. Give yourself a break! Be more balanced: draw up a list of your assets, strengths and personal resources. Be fair on yourself, and give yourself a 'good' talking to!

Self control: take ownership and responsibility for your actions, choices and decisions; don't blame others for your responses—choose them for yourself. Confidence comes from self belief, and a sense of control.

20
SELF CONTROL:
It takes real skill!

Self control: self control allows you to calmly and rationally exercise choice, choose your preferred response. It is therefore a high order skill; a true test of maturity.

When provoked, without self control we tend to knee-jerk a reaction, react emotionally rather than rationally. Good management usually requires a reasoned response, rather than an emotional one—hence the importance of self control.

The essence of self control is taking 'time out' to think, consider and reflect, before taking action; to insert 'pause' between the external provocation and your internal response. This pause is then used to allow you to choose your response, rather than simply react.

Ways in which you can press your pause button include:

Ask yourself: "what alternatives do I have here?": this forces you to consider options—the essence of a rational decision. Also, in thinking about these options, then weighing them, the 'emotional' surge will pass, and you will calm down

Ask yourself: "How will what I'm about to do look at 11 pm tonight?": this turns your attention to consequences of your action, rather than the action itself. A mature decision is one in which consequences of actions are considered; immature decisions are ones in which only the actions seem to count....

Self protection: as a manager you may come up against difficult members of staff who are in effect, immovable objects. Whatever you do or try, they persist with their difficult behaviours. In the worst case scenario, their motivation is to be difficult, and in particular, to make your life as difficult as possible as their manager... In such circumstances, ensure you protect yourself. Do not let them take you down, emotionally, and do not resort to behaving as they do. If either of these things happen, you will cease to behave in a professional way, and they will have 'won'.

So:

- Act with integrity at all times; maintain your own high standards; take pride in your professionalism
- Take ownership of who you are, and how you behave; never hear yourself say 'they are making me....': make yourself!
- Always be a positive role model: take pride in being as good as you can be in the worst of circumstances

- Ensure that you always—always—treat that member of staff as professionally as you do any other of your team. Ensure there is no marginalising, or offloading, or any other unprofessional behaviour

- Tomorrow is another day—who knows: if you continue to be positive, helpful and professional, this may be the day that you start to have a positive impact on that individual….

- Have constructive ways of offloading any stress; above all, don't be infected by their negativity: inoculate yourself…!

21
STAYING CALM

Professionally, as a manager, you will need to stay calm, or at the very least, appear calm, in any difficult situation. Easier said than done....... so some suggestions as to how to do it

- Breathe: take a deep breath (right down in your tummy), and let it out slowly—then repeat. This provides a good oxygen supply to your heart and bloodstream, relaxes muscles, and helps your brain process more effectively

- **Pause**: take a time out; don't rush in with a decision or response. Make sure that what you say, or what you do, is a choice, made from at least two options. By giving yourself options you are buying time, and this in itself helps you get through the 'anxiety' surge

- Move from anxiety to problem solving: this is a reframing technique that can be very effective. It consists of 3 key steps:

1: recognise, physically, that you are getting anxious (stomach churning)

2: create a 'program interrupt' that forces you to recognise you are getting anxious, and which tells you to stop (eg a picture, or a sound, or some other signal you can easily recall).Associate this signal with your physical symptom, so that every time you have the symptom, you recall

3: use the signal to switch to problem solving mode. What is the problem? Why is it a problem? What are my options? Which do I prefer? Do it! Whilst problem solving, your brain will be focused on this, and stop sending out anxiety signals...

22
STRESS:
5 magic steps to stress release

Stress management can be divided into two parts: stress prevention and stress release:

Prevention:

> 1: EVENT
> 2: PERCEPTION
> 3: MENTAL RESPONSE
> 4: CHEMICAL RELEASE

Release:

> 5: PHYSICAL RESPONSE

Prevention:

1: event: if you know an event is likely to be difficult, either remove yourself from it, do what you can to avoid it, or minimise or remove those parts of the event that you find difficult or problematic

2: perception: your stress may be less to do with the external event, than with your internal response to it—especially the way you see it. This tends to be a self-fulfilling prophesy—ie seek and you will find. If you are inclined (especially subconsciously) to 'see' or anticipate something as difficult or problematic, then that is the likely outcome. So try changing how you see things, or how you look at something (or someone). See if you can find the upside or benefit in the situation.

One typical example of this element is your inner voice:

Your inner voice (internal dialogue) is often programmed to protect you, but at times this can work against you, by being too cautious or restrictive ("be careful", "don't risk it", "it will go wrong"). So be prepared to challenge this voice, and even replace it with a more constructive, more positive, inner dialogue ("what might be the benefit if I do it?", "what's good about this option/person?")

3: mental response: this is the most difficult stage to take ownership of, or alter—but it is possible, with determination and practice. In this stage, your mind has seen the event as a threat (stages 1 and 2), and is about to signal to your body—'prepare for action!'. At this point you can choose to respond differently—ie send a different signal to the rest of your body. So this stage is about self control and staying calm (see tip 21). The key point is this: your body cannot get stressed unless your mind gives it the go ahead. So even if the situation is difficult, practice mental control and calmness—ie make a choice to not get stressed.

4: chemical response: if at stage 3 your mind tells your body to 'go', then it triggers a set of bio-chemical responses in your body. Once this has happened, you are now committed to stress release, rather than stress prevention...

5: Stress release: there are essentially two types of release—positive and negative.

Negative release techniques are essentially self-destructive and unhealthy. They would typically include:

- withdrawing, becoming isolated; closing down
- developing unhelpful response/coping habits, from

tapping to excessive drinking/eating

- unspent nervous energy (part of the bio-chemical response) - leading to nervous exhaustion and/or lack of sleep
- expressing or releasing the energy in unhelpful ways for others — eg anger, irritation, moodiness, tearfulness

Positive release techniques are all to do with acknowledging the stress within, and getting rid of it quickly, and constructively. They would include:

- Exercise
- Relaxation
- Talking it through with someone (not 'dumping' your frustrations)
- Distraction—eg film, book, conversation—so you don't dwell on the problem. Particularly helpful if this involves laughter (a great stress reliever!)

The key point for stage 5 is that you have a choice. It is up to you a) to recognise you are stressed, and b) choose a destructive or constructive response.

23
BEING PERSUASIVE:
Try having a SKIVE

In any presentation—formal or informal— your success often depends on your ability to persuade. The quality of the case or argument itself is crucial; but so too are your own personal qualities and approach.

Success, in these terms, often depends on SKIVE:

S   success is:
K   knowing your material/subject
I   involving your audience
V   visually representing your ideas
E   enthusiasm for your topic or case

Knowledge and enthusiasm are two qualities that absolutely belong to you, and are controlled by you. The audience will expect you to be both, and your credibility will be enhanced (or diminished) accordingly.

Involving the audience works, because people are more attentive if involved, and remember better issues that they contributed to or participated in. Involvement can include questions, debate, small group work, case work, completing a quiz or questionnaire, or being entertained.

Visuals should be tied to the message, to make the message memorable. Visuals do three things: they grab attention; they help explain the point you are making; and they help people remember.

24
BOUNDARY SETTING:
Line in the sand

You will find it useful to set a clear boundary - a Line In The Sand (LITS). The boundary should clarify what is your responsibility, and what is the responsibility of the other person or group. Two key relationships that benefit from clear LITS are the relationship you have with your own manager, and that you have with your team and individuals within it. (Other possibilities peers, projects teams, partnerships, and even with your family).

You don't need a boundary on everything—it would be too complex. Instead, set a boundary on issues that are crucial for your relationship and performance, and to avoid overlap or gaps.

Without this line, you might take on work which isn't yours and others may take advantage of this—especially since you seem comfortable doing it. So you could end up feeling, and being, exploited—and overworked....

25
CONFLICT MANAGEMENT:
Lighten UP!

When in a new, challenging or difficult situation, the other person, or group, might appear to be very tense. Frowning, tight lipped, arms folded, quiet…. You could interpret this tension as hostility—towards the event, and/or towards you. As a consequence, we might respond by becoming defensive, or even aggressive—which only reinforces their tension, and might even generate hostility.

However, the reason for their tense appearance is often anxiety: they are unsure about the event, and possibly fear what might happen, or what you are going to say, or how you are going to react. If this is the case, the best approach you can take is to **reassure** them—put them at ease. Remember too, that you might appear tense to them—which they might take as hostility, rather than anxiety. So do your best not to carry an appearance of tension into the meeting or event.

26
FACILITATION:
What is it?

Facilitation is a long word for 'help'. A facilitator's role is to help—not take over.

In facilitating a meeting, your role is to focus on process, and let the meeting membership focus on content. In other words, you manage how the meeting is run; they focus on what the meeting is about.

In many ways, it is best not to be an expert in the meeting content; that way, you are unlikely to contribute to the content debate, and instead are free to focus on process issues, which include:

- ensuring there is an agenda, and that it is stuck to
- keeping to time
- ensuring all ideas, suggestions, decisions and actions are recorded
- keeping the meeting focused and on track
- agreeing then maintaining 'ground rules' (ways in which this meeting wants to operate)
- addressing inappropriate behaviour though positive intervention

You can contrast the role of facilitator with that of leader: the leader might 'lead' on each item; give a lead for others to follow; and have the final say. The facilitator is more of a referee; ensuring the game is played properly, to the right rules; ensuring all goals are recorded; having no bias to either side; and maintaining discipline....

27
FACILITATOR:
To be a great one...

- agree your role and responsibilities—and theirs—at the outset

- if appropriate, set some ground rules for the code conduct of the meeting; this gives you your authority. If you have to intervene you will be doing so to maintain the code

- know the names of the group members—it helps establish and maintain rapport

- be the group recorder, using a flip chart (or powerpoint); this way everyone can see what's being recorded

- use their words when recording; if you want to summarise, ask their permission

- never take decisions on behalf of the meeting; it is their meeting. Be prepared to raise a critical issue, then offer choices. If you take the decision, you will be accountable for it in their eyes, and it helps them avoid responsibility. For example, if they are over-running, offer the choice of continuing to over-run, or closing it down, and point out the consequence of each option and remember the decision is theirs

- if you want to speak on the item, ask someone else to facilitate that item

- sit or stand to signal 'taking back control': sitting implies you are ok with discussion; standing and moving to the flip chart will signal you want the discussion to stop....

28
FACILITATION:
Stepping in!

If someone's behaviour is proving counter-productive, and you feel it is your role to intervene, consider the following approach.

Firstly—is it best tackled outside the meeting—ie in private, rather than in public. If so, you could have a word before or after the meeting, or call a break and have a word then

However, if you need to intervene 'there and then', the following 10-point strategy might help:

1. Think first: what's the problem, and why is it a problem (consequences); this means you will focus on the issue, and not the individual

2. Think second: what do you want to say (message), and how do you want to say it (tone); write it down, if it helps

3. Ensure you are calm and in control; breathe deeply and slowly, and relax

4. Choose your moment: even if the person is dominating, they will have to pause for breath at some time; try to avoid interrupting, but if you have to, apologise, then get on with it..

5. Use their name, as a softener

6. Acknowledge their contribution (be genuine)

7. Raise your concern, and why it is a concern

8. Suggest your preferred alternative

9. Seek visual approval from the rest (you should get it)

10. Thank the group, and move on

An example of stepping in:

Suppose someone is very knowledgeable, and what they are saying is valid, but it is excluding others from contributing, and they are getting frustrated.

1. The problem is lack of contribution from others, which is not only frustrating for them, but it means the meeting is not getting a full range of opinions to consider. (Making it a problem for others, avoids direct criticism of the speaker, and its impact on the meeting depersonalises any issue)

2. I'm going to use these words "........", and speak in a calm, measured tone, with a brightness/confidence to my tone—sound self-assured

3. Take a few deep breaths

4. Wait for him to pause...and:

5. "David......(just before you continue)

6. What you've said is very helpful/valuable (summarise quickly if you feel it will help)

7. I'm aware there are others who want to contribute or pick up on what you've said so far. I'm keen to ensure everyone who wants to can have say

8. So can I ask you to hold it there for a moment, whilst I bring in a couple of people who I know want to say something?

9. (Scanning the meeting) Is that OK with everyone? David?

10. Thanks. OK...Jennifer, I think you.......

29
FOUNDATIONS FOR RELATIONS:
The Formulae

Most of us would really like positive relationships with others. Unfortunately, we tend not to spend time in building such relationships—either because we are too busy, or too task-focused (rather than relationship focused), or because we don't really know the basis for a good relationship. There are three key building blocks that underpin positive relationships. The continuing presence of these three maintain a positive relationship; the lack of any or all of these three make positive relationships very difficult, if not impossible.

Trust + respect + value

Trust: good, positive relationships are based on mutual trust. Essentially people will trust you if you do what you say you will do, and not do what you say you won't do. Essentially trust is built through integrity: honouring your word.

Respect: you will be respected if you are not only trustable, but also credible. Credibility comes from your reputation and track record, and also your value system (see below).

Value: you not only have a consistent and demonstrable set of values, which the other person can respect (especially if those are shared values), but you also respect the value base of others (even if you don't agree with them). Above all, you also value the individual (through, for instance, trust and respect)

30
FEEDBACK:
It's about give and take!

GIVING FEEDBACK - PLEASE Praise:

- don't be shy; everyone likes praise
- make sure the praise relates to something specific, and...
- ...to something they were responsible for
- offer the praise as close to the incident as possible

If you need to give critical feedback:

- only give feedback on things the person can change or do something about and
- be constructive by making the feedback about behaviour, not personality or attitude
- give examples to be specific
- choose an appropriate place and time
- give the feedback as close to the incident as possible
- find anything good in the incident, and refer to it
- consider this 4 step approach:
1. identify the situation or incident
2. describe their behaviour
3. identify/explain the (negative) impact of that behaviour
4. suggest an alternative—or get them to

RECEIVING FEEDBACK:

- listen
- take notes if it helps
- say thank you at the end of the feedback
- offer a view there and then, or, if you prefer, take it away to think about
- don't be defensive, you'll not get feedback again

31
IMPRESSION MANAGEMENT -
The Five Factors

There are 5 ways in which you create an impression on others.

1. how you look

2. how you sound

3. how you act, or behave.

All of the above are covered earlier. We 'radiate' impressions all the time through these three. In fact, it is impossible not to make an impression—so the only questions are:

Do I care?   And if I do….

What impression do I want to make?

All three of these belong to you, and are under your control— you can 'be' however you want in these three areas.

In order to create a positive impression, all you really have to do is 'be positive' in these three areas—ie look positive, sound positive, and behave/act in a positive manner. Think of people you like and respect, and who you're happy to spend time with; then think of the opposite. Chances are, the first group will be positive in these three outlets, and the opposites will not. If you decide to be positive in these three areas, then something else will happen that's very beneficial—you will actually start to feel better about yourself. As you 'behave' positively externally, you are more likely to feel positive, too—ie your external self can shape your internal self.

The other two ways of making an impression are

4. reputation

5. your category.

Reputation goes ahead of you. In that sense, you cannot directly control it—it belongs 'out there', with others. However, you are responsible for those actions of yours which create your reputation.

The main point is that however you are now, in your interactions with others, will contribute to your reputation; and people may actually judge you first by your reputation— because your reputation runs ahead of you.

If our reputation is good, it helps in any interaction; if it is poor, it acts as a block or barrier to that interaction.

Category follows on from the above. Though you exist as yourself, you belong to a wide range of categories: gender, race, age, likes, dislikes, hobbies, and so on. In any relationship with others, they might (subconsciously) put you in a category.

If they do, then how they work with you partly depends on how they judge that category. If their view of the category is bad, it won't help in your relationship; if it is good, it will. So the skill is to be sensitive to your categories, watch and listen for being 'labelled' (categorised) in an unhelpful way, and ensure you position yourself in a category that is true, but helpful to your relationship.

32
INFLUENCING STRATEGIES:
Do you take £'s?

Currencies, cues and clues

As someone living in the UK, you are used to spending in pounds sterling (£). If you were to go on holiday or business to most of Europe, you would expect to take Euros (€). If you insisted in taking £s, you might struggle...in other words, you'll find it easier to get what you want if you spend in their currency.

The same principle applies to influencing people: if you want to get what you want, find out what their currency is . All this means is—discover what they prefer or like, and do your best to work with these preferences.

They can be style currencies, for example they like ideas and information presented in a formal structured way with detail, or informally; they may prefer overview and idea only through discussion. You can also use peoples interests as currency to influence, for example using an anecdote about sport to explain a proposal or problem.

If you work with or in their currencies, things they connect with, you are more likely to have rapport and influence. This is only true if you show genuine interest in the other person and their currencies—rather than dominate them with your own.

Look and listen for clues and cues to their currencies, you need to be on the lookout for them. So get them talking, and listen carefully for their cues and clues to their currencies.

33
INFLUENCING:
I could get to like you

Two key factors
Credibility and Likeability

Credibility is based on your track record. This is not only how well you've done, but also the kind of person you are. It is the basis of your reputation. Do you have a reputation for achieving things? Do you have a reputation for sticking to your word (integrity)?

Think of people who have been, or continue to be, influential. They are likely to be credible to you. This credibility is likely to be a combination of what they have done, and who they are: their human doing record, and their human being record.

We tend to be influenced by people we like. There is also a view that we tend to like people who are like us. This second factor is covered on the previous page, through currencies.

In terms of 'being liked', it is possible—even necessary—for others to like you, or at least feel comfortable with you, if you want to influence them positively. So act as you would to and with a friend. No need to 'be everyone's friend'; just act in a friend-ly way with people—it pays off. So think how you are with a friend, and things you would do for a friend and then think of the effect this would have on others e.g. Listen to a friend? listen to others. Talk to a friend? Talk to others. Be open with friends? Be open with others...

34
INFLUENCING:
Can I get you a drink?

Reciprocity

If you are in a group having a drink, and someone else buys the first round, which includes a drink for you – do you feel a strong obligation to take your turn, and buy another round? If someone pays you a compliment, do you typically (and without thinking) often pay a compliment back?

If a salesman makes you a special offer, or puts themselves out for you, does it make you more inclined to buy the product or service?

One of the most powerful influencing tools is reciprocity – the feeling most people have to 'pay back' a favour granted by someone else. This is sometimes referred to as 'indebtedness'.

Key points to remember:

- You may unintentionally create a sense of indebtedness; so if someone offers to pay—accept it, and if you prefer, give the payment to a charity—or suggest they do the same. This will clear the debt and also reinforce the genuineness of your gift

- If you feel indebted by someone else's favour, either insist on paying—or donating to charity—or accept it genuinely as a gift—ie with no burden of reciprocity. In other words, the nature of a gift is that it has no sense of reciprocal obligation...

35
INTER-PERSONAL SKILLS:
How do you measure up?

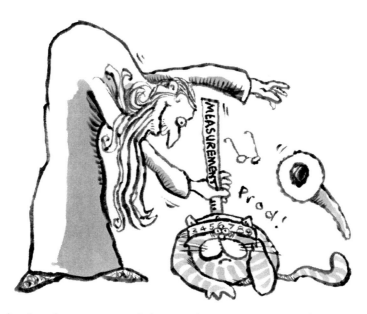

Whole books can, and have, been written about inter-personal skills (IPS).

Our top 10 are:

1. Active listening
2. Questioning and probing
3. Acknowledging
4. Building
5. Summarising and recapping
6. Creating empathy and rapport
7. Being other centred
8. Using language sensitively
9. Befriending
10. Climate control

Ask someone you work to score you out of 10 against the description of these skills on the next few pages (10=Excellent) and compare against your own view

Active listening: showing that you are listening, through such things as eye contact, nodding, posture, body language, and the ability to clarify, summarise and recap

Questioning and probing: knowing when to ask open and closed questions; avoiding multiple, complex and leading questions; and ensuring you follow up on vague or ambiguous answers with appropriate probing questions (eg "can you give me an example...?"; "when was the last time...?")

Acknowledging: showing you value the other person and their contributions—eg by knowing their name, and using it, but echoing back comments or words they've used, or by agreeing with them—explicity, rather than in your head

Building: an important form of acknowledgement, in which you accept the other person's idea or comment and build on it—thus both supporting it and adding value to it

Summarising and recapping: the most important form of active listening, and also a way of keeping the meeting or conversation focused. It is also an excellent way of regaining control if the conversation or meeting is slipping away from you

Creating empathy and rapport: this can be done, subtly, in a number of ways—by mirroring (not mimicking) the other person's body language, pace, language and tone, so that you are 'in synch' with them

Being other centred: thinking all the time "how is this for them?". Our first thought is often "how does this suit me?" - eg time and location for a meeting—but sometimes it might be worthwhile putting yourself out to put the other person in

Using language sensitively: the devil is often in the detail: pay attention to some of the small things that can make a big difference. For example:

> directive **v** collaborative language
>
> inclusive **v** excluding language
>
> can do **v** can't do language
>
> 'either/or' **v** 'and'
>
> statements **v** questions
>
> my point of view **v** your point of view
>
> short **v** long words/sentences

See 'micro behaviours' tip 39

Befriending: this involves behaving in a friendly manner, whatever the other person is doing or like. Act with everyone much as you would act with a friend

Climate control: every meeting or conversation has a prevailing mood, atmosphere or climate. You are responsible for setting the best climate, noticing if it is poor, and intervening to change it.

For example:

unhelpful	helpful
problem focused	solution focused
taking separate positions	sharing common interests

past	present or future
what we can't do	what we can do
defending	building
telling	collaborating

36
LEADERSHIP:
How would you lead your ship?

This page offers two classic views of leadership:

leadership as 'headship' (or position)

leadership as 'attributional' (or characteristics)

Headship:

In this view, leadership lies at the head of any organisation or unit—the place where ultimate authority for that organisation or unit rests. 3 factors seem crucial for successful leadership in this position: clarity, positive intervention, and profiling.

Clarity involves such things as providing initial and ongoing direction: setting and endorsing a clear vision and mission, and ways of how to get there, and how the organisation should operate, ethically (ie a combination of what, why and how). It is also about resolving or removing ambiguity and uncertainty at difficult times.

Positive intervention involves the leader 'stepping in and stepping up' in times of crisis, change, or when there are difficult decisions to be made that affect the whole organisation and its workforce.

Profiling is the ambassadorial role of headship; the visible face of the company or unit; they need to be visible, and aligned—ie their individual self must align with the values and identity of the company they head. They must be a positive role model for the organisation; its positive public face.

Attributional leadership:

In this view, leadership is all about having a particular set of qualities or attributes, that together, help create a successful leader. In this view, leaders can, do and should emerge at any point in the organisation.

From this perspective, the following 5 characteristics are often thought the most important:

Sense of timing: simply, being in the right place at the right time. Knowing when to intervene, and doing so

Courage: the courage of conviction, and the bravery to speak up and speak out. This tends to be a vital factor in gathering a support base, or in representing one. It is closely associated with integrity—making a stand for what you believe to be right

Vision: the ability to look up, to look out, and to look ahead; to see the desired future—and ideally how to get there

Passion: such leaders have conviction—a strong set of principles and beliefs, and a willingness to share them with others. They need to be able to communicate this passion well

Resonance: such leaders must be able to strike a chord and identify with those they lead; there must be some commonality—of values, ambition, direction; some personal appeal

37
MANAGEMENT STYLE:
Where does it come from?

Style is the result of three factors: context, personal preference and skills.

PERSONAL STYLE

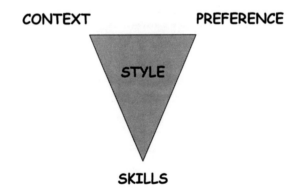

CONTEXT   PREFERENCE

STYLE

SKILLS

Context: the situation faced by the manager, including, organisational culture, and how others prefer to work. Different strokes for different folks! There are other situations that make a difference. For example, time: managers who are short of time tend to be more directive, since collaboration tends to take more time.

Personal preference: we often adopt a style, like a favourite piece of clothing, that feels most comfortable. Very often we will choose (unconsciously) that which we feel most comfortable or familiar with—even if it isn't particularly appropriate.

Skills: clearly a manager is more likely to choose a style which matches his or her skills set; for example, a collaborative style benefits from someone who is comfortable with managing discussion, chairing and facilitation skills

In general, it is the mix of these three factors that determine the overall style chosen. Clearly the style will therefore change as the three factor mix changes.

However, the two factors of personal preference and skills tend to reinforce each other: the better you are at it, the more likely you are to be comfortable with it; and the more comfortable you are with it, the more likely you are to choose it as a style, and therefore improve your skills.

Beware! At its worst, you might choose a style for due to comfort and preference, when in fact it should be the context (including what would work for the other person or people concerned) that ought to be the dominating factor.

38
MANAGERS INFLUENCE:
5 styles

When intervening in any situation, think consciously about the style you wish to use. Of course, in a complex situation, you might need to use a combination of styles as the situation and dynamics alter.

TELL

　　　　SELL

　　　　　　　　NEGOTIATE

　　　　　　　　　　　COLLABORATE

　　　　　　　　　　　　　　　FACILITATE

Directive-Push　　　　　　　　　Non-directive-Pull

Tell: most directive, top down; autocratic; often relies on authority; other person or group tend to be passive; non-consultative; very controlling; can be quick and decisive

Sell: uses persuasion, influence and selling skills; tries to bring other person to their point of view; still has a 'win' in mind

Negotiate: bargaining and trading skills to the fore; conversation built around 'if...then'; good at flexibility and compromise—seeking a win-win where all parties gain an advantage.

Collaborate: joint problem solving; bringing all stakeholders together; consultative, more democratic, more involving; can be slower and can seem indecisive

Facilitate: simply helping the other person, or group, to come to its own decisions; hands off; trusting the abilities and commitments of the other person/team

No one style is or should be dominant; they will all be required at some time or other by any manager. It is worth reflecting on whether you have a tendency or preference for one or other of these styles—and conversely, whether you tend to avoid or feel uncomfortable with any of them.

Make it a conscious choice!

39
MICRO LANGUAGE -
It's not what you say..

Micro behaviours refer to the very small differences that you can make and that can really work for or against you in any conversation. Here are just a few examples..

Using either/or versus and: if you use of 'either/or' you force a choice, and therefore sets up a 'win/lose' outcome—either A or B. Using 'and' instead allows both options to happen or be considered—a win win outcome. So if offered either A or B just challenge to see if 'and' meaning both can work just as well, or better.

Statements v questions: in any conversation, monitor how many of your sentences end in a full stop, and how many end in a question mark. This will reveal how often you use statements, which are telling/directive, and how often you ask questions, which are including and collaborative. For example ... "it is...!" ... or "is it that...?" can have a different tone in a conversation

QP v R: some people can be quick processors (QP) some reflectors (R). Quick processors often talk quite quickly, respond and process information quickly, although not always appropriately or accurately. At their extreme, QPs have a tendency to dominate and to interrupt or finish other peoples sentences off!

Reflectors usually listen fully to the statement, then work out their response—it is often measured. They usually talk more slowly with pauses, and can appear less engaged or enthusiastic They may struggle to be heard, since QPs respond more quickly and others may get frustrated waiting...

Imagine a meeting with QP's and R's ... they can of course get really frustrated with each other. QP's need to be aware and adjust accordingly, likewise for R's.

So in any meeting, including one-to-ones, a QP and R may not work well together, and each criticise the other, mentally, for their inappropriate behaviour: (a QP may feel Rs are passengers in meetings; Rs may feel QPs are dominating and inconsiderate).

As a good manager you can try and take these micro behaviours into account. There are several ways to do this:

- Understand that 'inappropriate behaviour' may be lack of self awareness, rather than anything deliberate

- It's clearly not just what you say, but how you say it, that makes a difference

- Be sensitive to others' responses to how you say things, and consider changing your approach if things are not going well

- Put some of these ideas into your consciousness. It may seem difficult and even contrived at first, but it will improve with practice, particularly if you are motivated to improve and can see the benefit—after all, that's how most of us learned something equally as complex and difficult at first—driving a car!

and that's what gets results!

40
MOTIVATION:
Spell number 6A!

Everyone is responsible for their own motivation. But the manager can and should do what they can to promote things that can motivate, and minimise the demotivators that affect people.

This diagram shows the 6 factors crucial to anyone's motivation.

THE 6As

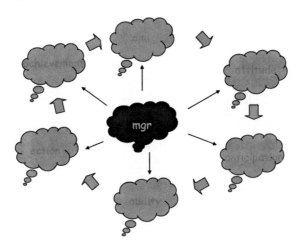

All 6 are necessary in order to be successfully motivated. If any one is missing, the person will not be motivated. In the above diagram, the individual owns the 6As—and they can make these happen with or without a manager (hence self-motivation).

The manager can work to build and sustain each of the 6 As.

Aim: to be motivated you need a purpose, goal, aim, ambition

Attitude: you need to see a benefit, or a value, in that aim or goal

Anticipation: you need to believe the goal is achievable

Ability: you have to have the resources and wherewithal— knowledge, skills, good health, time

Action: you must be prepared to do something; put in effort

Achievement: nothing succeeds like success; you need regular and relatively quick payback or payoff, to justify the effort

So, as a **manager support** each of those 6 As by:

Aim: ensure they are clear; consider long and short term goals and possibly bite size chunks

Attitude: ensure there is something of value in it for them or those they care about; people can be motivated by either the process of the work and the outcome (achievement, result)

Anticipation: do what you can to build confidence and belief e.g. by reference to previous achievements

Ability: provide knowledge and help them develop skills through training and development, or through personal coaching and consider learning style and preference

Action: you may want to use incentives, or positive reinforcement strategies; you may want to act as their conscience, and provide reminders and gentle 'prods'; offer praise and encouragement for every step achieved

Achievement: acknowledge, praise and celebrate!

You can use the 6As to both think through and prepare for a meeting, and to help structure a discussion.

41
MOTIVATION –
Content & process

People may be just as motivated (or demotivated) by process- how things are done as by content-what it is they have to do?

So in managing staff and workloads, consider the how as much as you consider the what

Often there is more flexibility in the 'how' anyway; two people might have the identical job description, but will do it in different ways.

Talk with your staff to discuss and discover different ways of doing the job that might appeal to them: maximise what works for them, and minimise what doesn't.

Process variables to consider include:

- Location-e.g. working from home
- Flexible hours- including times in the week
- Their preference for being managed-how 'hands on' or 'hands off' do they want you to be
- Working with others or working alone
- Degree of rigidity to follow,versus degree of autonomy/discretion

In all of these, don't assume:ask. Everyone is different, and needs change within individuals from task to task over time.

42
MOTIVATION – Hard & soft

Think of the typical resources you manage.

Chances are, you'll have included some of the following:

     Money
     Staff/labour
     Equipment
     Materials
     Time
     Space/accommodation
     Information

These are what we call hard, or external resources.

Hard in the sense that they are tangible, concrete, measurable, and eventually, will erode or diminish in value (staff can get tired....)

External in that they don't belong to you as the manager. The most you can do with such resources is:

Lobby for more or what you need

Look after them properly

Allocate them fairly

Now consider this definition of a motivational resource:

"anything of value to the other person that you can give or withhold"

Consider what you would include under this definition.

You are likely to come up with some of the following:

- Support
- Praise/feedback
- Encouragement
- Clear direction
- Fairness, openness, honesty
- Valuing the individual
- Appreciation and acknowledgement
- Trust, respect
- Showing an interest
- Making development opportunities available
- Access to you

These are known as soft, or internal, resources.

Soft in that they are intangible, hard to measure, but no less important for that.

Internal because they all belong to you: they come from you—you own them.

The great news is that most staff really value these soft, internal resources—and know that the best managers can deliver. Consider the worst manager you have experienced. Was the worst good or bad on soft resources? How about the best manager you had ? The chances are, that they were generous with the soft stuff…..

So….

       ….be generous with the 'soft' stuff.

43
MOTIVATION:
Incentive or Reward?

Incentive and Reward: are they the same?

Incentives are offered ahead of the task, as inducement or encouragement.

Rewards are offered afterwards, as a form of recognition.

Incentives and rewards therefore can create a different psychological contract with the individual.

Incentives tend to emphasise the power relationship— ie "do it because I can offer something I have that you want" - at its worst, it could be seen as a bribe, and have a demeaning effect on the individual, and on the relationship between the individual and the person offering the incentive. Moreover, the incentive is most likely to produce a calculative response, rather than true motivation; the individual is doing it for the external, extrinsic benefit of the incentive, rather than the intrinsic worth of the task itself.

Reward, coming after the event, recognises the individual, their value, contribution and worth. As such, it values the individual, and tends to act more as a motivator. If I were offered more money to do what I do—as a motivator—I'd feel demeaned (I already am motivated). So the extra money would not touch my motivation: but a genuine 'thank you' afterwards would really give me a motivational lift....

44
MOTIVATION:
Values Agreement

Most 1-1 discussions between managers and staff focus on the workload and specific tasks. This technique focuses on the relationship between manager and staff.

It works like this:

1. Set up a 1-1 meeting, the outcome for which will be an agreed set of behaviours that each would value from the other.

2. Both you as manager and staff member prepare a list of things you would value from the other

3. At the meeting, the staff member reads their list; the manager notes it down, and responds with yes, no or 'let's discuss that further' to each item on the list

    - 'yes' means a commitment to deliver that behaviour

    - no means the manager won't or can't—and explains why

    - 'let's discuss' happens when the request is either too broad, or needs clarifying or qualifying

4. The process is reversed—ie the manager reads out their list, and the staff member responds

5. At the end of the process, both manager and staff member will have made clear commitments to deliver key behaviours valued by the other party

The manager's list (to read out):

"These are the 6 things I would most value and appreciate from you as a member of my team"

The staff member's list (to read out):

"These are the 6 things I would most value and appreciate from you as my manager"

Should you do this, you will find that most of your answers to their requests are 'yes'. This is because they ask for internal, soft resources (see tip 42), which belong to you. So the very things they say they value most from you, are yours to deliver!

The process can also work well with the whole team—since the team might have things they value as a team, which would not emerge from individual 1-1 meetings.

45
NEGATIVITY: The 4 types

They are:

- Stress release
- Cultural
- Genuine cause for concern
- Game player

Stress release: such people use negativity as a way of releasing pressure—they often 'go off' like a bottle of pop—but shortly afterwards, are fine again. So most of the time they are OK—but prone to occasional bouts of letting off steam

Cultural: negativity can become a habit; often it's easier to join in than make a stand (it also seems that negativity is more infectious than positivity—it seems it is easier to suck others in to expressing negativity than it is to expressing positivity). So for a lot of people, they aren't inherently negative—it's just 'how we are around here' - ie typically we moan, grumble, etc

Genuine cause for concern: this splits into two further types—aggrieved and demoralised. In both cases, the proper supportive attention might well pull them round

Game player: the most difficult to manage; for these people, they have consciously chosen to be negative, as a way of making life difficult for others—and particularly their manager. In fact, they are happy negatives—they enjoy and relish the discomfort they cause.

Each needs a different response.

45
NEGATIVITY:
Coping with the 4

Stress release: so long as this is not in public, or damaging to others, it is actually quite cathartic. As a manager, encourage the person to let off steam safely either on their own, or with you. Encourage them not to do it with others who will not appreciate it—including family

Cultural: you need to be a role model of positivity, and work to create a positive work culture. The 'Fish!' series of books have some good ideas in this respect

Genuine cause for concern: address the cause, and you address the effect. If they have a legitimate grievance, address it quickly, professionally and positively. For demoralised staff, find out why they are down; it is sometimes to do with external issues, and sometimes with internal perceptions (eg lack of confidence or low self esteem)

Game players: you need to understand this person well, on two levels: firstly, their (internal) motivation; and secondly, their (external) strategies. How you respond depends on the nature of each game player's motivation and behaviours. Firstly, let them know you are on to them—you can do this subtly, not confrontationally; secondly, refuse to be drawn into game playing; and above all, try to win their respect. The good news about game players is they are usually intelligent—so they are a real asset if you can turn them around...

46
NEGOTIATION:
Negotiation Matrix

Prepare for a negotiation by imagining you are about to negotiate with a paint and decorating company for work inside your house

	VARIABLE 1 (eg price)	VARIABLE 2 (eg deadline)	VARIABLE 3 (eg number of rooms)
IDEAL OPENING			
FALL BACKS			
BOTTOM LINE			

The matrix encourages you to identify two crucial sets of information, before you start to negotiate:

VARIABLES

Variables: all the factors inherent in the negotiation that can be varied. The examples given are only three of literally scores of variables that exist. In fact, most things are variable—ie can be more or less, sooner or later, bigger or smaller, higher or lower. A good negotiation principle is: negotiate anything that you are not happy with—ie at least try to turn it into a variable.

Why?

Because the essence of negotiation is to cross trade variables—rather than concede them. In other words, for everything the other party wants, be prepared to trade, rather than concede. So the more variables you can identify (for you and the other party), the more flexibility (and thus power) you have in the negotiation.

POSITION

Always start with the best outcome you can imagine. It's unlikely you'll get it unless you ask for it! Then work out the fall back positions you are prepared to go to, and ultimately your bottom line (on each variable) - ie your minimum. Then start with your ideal, and cross trade variables—so as you move down the grid, you should be gaining something in return. Remember that achieving all your bottom lines is a win; anything more is a bonus...!

SHAKE!

47
NEGOTIATION: Hints and tips

- Anything you are unhappy with you should attempt to negotiate

- Ask: are you prepared to negotiate on this? This lets you know straight away whether the other person understands negotiation, and has flexibility on their opening position

- The more variables you can identify, the more flexibility you will have

- Establish their priorities: there is more flexibility in the negotiation if you each have different priorities; you are more likely to get stuck if a) you share the same priority, and b) you can't find many variables in the negotiation

- Haggling is not negotiation—it is trying to find an acceptable outcome around a single variable that doesn't look like a variable to each party (eg price). But as soon as you find a new variable, you can negotiate (trade) and stop haggling

- Good negotiators are creative, and think on their feet; keep searching for variables

- It may be useful to have two meetings: the first, to discover the other party's situation, position, variables and priorities; the second, to conduct the negotiation

- Be prepared to walk away if your bottom lines are not met

- Use key interpersonal skills and information to establish credibility and likeability; don't be aggressive or attack: seek a win-win

Put your best negotiator in; don't negotiate yourself, if you are a poor negotiator...

48
PERSUASION:
Words of WiZdom!

Persuasion is really selling, which is best describes as helping someone to buy.

At any time you may be required to sell 5 things:

- product
- service
- proposal
- idea
- yourself

The tips that follow relate to all the above, equally.

- In order to sell, you need to achieve one or more of these:

    - meet a need

    - solve a problem

    - generate a desire/want

- sell the **benefits**, not features: if you were selling your house, and had a large garden, then that is a feature of your house. It only becomes a **benefit** to the purchaser if they find a large garden attractive. For some people, a large garden would be an obstacle or objection (too much work)

- sell PIs, not the product: a PI is a performance indicator – an aspect or characteristic of the product, service or proposal that is important to the customer. For example see a camera as possible PIs of; price, ease of use, lightness, versatility, etc.

People look at the PIs, and use these to discriminate one product from the others. So find out what PIs matter most to the purchaser.

- Hold a conversation first, to find out what the other person actually needs or wants, and what their problems or concerns are. Don't assume these will be the same as yours and don't guess, find out.

- Explicit/implicit: some needs and wants are clearly expressed by the purchaser and they are happy to talk about them; other needs, equally important, are implicit – either the purchaser isn't consciously aware of them, or are reluctant to admit to them (eg aspects that meet status, power, ego needs/ wants).

- Clues & cues: listen carefully, and observe reactions, and do some homework, to discover some of these implicit needs and wants – what is the evidence for any such implicit needs – eg what do they seem to value through how they are, how they dress, their hobbies, interest, lifestyle, etc.

- Anticipate, then overcome, objections: specific objections, if you get them early enough, are good news, in that they are actually unmet needs. They tell you where your offer is failing; so you know which gaps you have to close. Then, when you have closed them, it is very difficult for the purchaser not to buy. The worst objection is one that is unspecific – "thanks, but no…". Always find out the detailed objection.

49

STAFF DEVELOPMENT-
Developing the apprentice

You may have a formal role in terms of appraisals or Performance Review and Development (PRD), often ending up in the completion of a Personal Development Plan (PDP). But consider the following, all of which represent good management practice in this area:

- Follow up on PDP: many staff are sceptical and cynical about PDPs because the process seems to stop once the form has been completed. Keep them up to date on progress.

- If you identify an area for development distinguish between a bid and a commitment. A bid is something that can only be met outside your remit – ie you are bidding for this development need to be met by putting it to HR for their consideration/approval. A commitment is something that you can take personal responsibility for making happen.

- You as a manager often have more ability to 'make development' happen, a lot more than you think.

- Development is much more than 'training' – it includes coaching, mentoring, reading, discussion, shadowing, rotation, visits, and so on. Such development is often less costly, more flexible, more timely and more relevant than a 'training course'.

50
TEAM BUILDING:
Team types

It's worth knowing that there are essentially four team types:

- project team
- co-ordination or liaison team
- culture team
- social teams
- Project team: all members of the team know they are working on a common project, something that has a clear start and finish time. There will usually be a clear project brief to work to, and project roles for the team members. Typically this team will spend considerable time together, working on a shared result or goal. The key skills needed for this team are project management skills.
- Co-ordination/liaison team: most members of this team typically do not meet together frequently; they are free standing, working on their own, in their separate areas – occasionally consulting each other. But occasionally this group of people will formally meet together (eg twice a term) to do some of the following:
  - o Make shared decisions
  - o Discuss common concerns or problems
  - o Keep each other up to date

This group rarely meet and they have much less sense of an identity and less of a collective commitment to the team.

The main skill needed in these teams are meeting skills – because typically they only operate as a team in such settings.

- Cultural team: members of these teams rarely work together as a single team. Their members are often free standing, getting on with their own jobs. The sense of belonging to a team comes from sharing a set of norms, values, principles and ethics, as well as (though not necessarily) shared goals and purposes. It's these shared norms that give the team members their sense of inclusion and belonging, and helps keep the team spirit alive.

The key skills here are sharing common values, norms and beliefs – for these are the glue that keep such teams together.

- Social team: this is really a sub-set of the previous type. Social teams enjoy each others' company, and spend time socially (usually informally) together. They like each other, and are essentially friendship groups. Such friendship teams get along well together, but (as an element in other, larger teams) can provide a different focus, and even (as a clique) undermine the whole team.

So if you wanted someday to build your team, it is worth thinking about what kind of team you want to build. Generally speaking, time invested in cultural, value-based teams is worthwhile, since it then provides a solid platform for that team becoming either a project team or a liaison team.

51
TEAM BUILDING:
As if by magic!

The Transformation Team

The idea for a Transformation Team builds on the work done by Meredith Belbin, and his idea of team roles.

Research shows that organisations that transform and significantly change and improve, usually have a range of players necessary for that success.

Typically there are 5 key roles required; though one person could provide all 5 roles, it is difficult and rare. Usually such transformation needs several people to be involved – hence the need for a team approach.

The 5 key roles are:

- Visionary
- Inventor
- Champion
- Resourcer
- Manager

Visionary: someone who can see the future – see what is required – but may not be able to see how to get there

Inventor: someone good at converting the vision into action; a problem solver; good at ideas and solutions – but may need the kick start of someone's ideas and vision to get them going

Champion: an enthusiast, a salesperson; someone who will get behind the idea and solution, and sell it to a bigger audience and market. A really good communicator

Resourcer: someone with either the resources or muscle to put into the venture, to make it happen; this could include having lots of influence, and being well networked

Manager: someone who, at the end of the process, will make the new 'state' (product or idea) work, regularly and reliably – will get it embedded, and surround it with good management procedures and structures to keep it on track

Some people can perform more than one role: for example, visionaries are often also champions, and can also be inventors.

However, good visionaries are very rarely good managers – and vice versa. This is because visionaries are looking ahead, whereas managers are focused on making the here and now work. Visionaries are risk takers and comfortable with uncertainty; managers tend to be the opposite.

52
TEAM BUILDING:
Creating the rules!

Code of conduct

It often helps teams to perform if they can agree a Code of Conduct to help the team work effectively. The Code of Conduct is often a mix of these three elements:

Values   Ground rules   Behaviours

Don't get hung up! One person's value can be another's behaviour. What is important is guidelines affecting behaviour can be very helpful in managing difficult dynamics effectively and maintaining team performance.

Values: a set of shared values, beliefs, principles and ethics that all team members sign up to supporting. They might include mutual respect; openness; commitment to the team

Ground rules: a set of procedures and frameworks that guide how the team will operate: could include; start and finish team meetings on time; rotating team leader

Behaviours: usually a mix of positive behaviours (which help) and negative behaviours (which hinder) – for example: not interrupting; building on others' contributions; staying focused.

It helps to have the team start with a blank sheet of paper, and discuss and agree the code themselves, rather than impose it.

The leader can then refer to it for their authority.

You'll be judged on
Getting Results

53
ACHIEVING RESULTS:
Start with OUTCOME

Output and outcome

OUTCOME	OUTPUT	ACTIVITY

An **activity** is what you or anyone else spends their time on at work

An **output** is the direct result of any activity; it is the produce produced, or the service delivered.

An **outcome** is the impact that product or service has on its intended market or customer.

So, this book is a product – it's an output from our activities (thinking, reading, researching, writing, editing).

The outcome of this book, however, is less easy to define. One outcome could be in terms of money generated by sales; another could be a direct improvement in your management, as a result of reading this.

Outputs are controlled by the organisation, and outcomes are influenced by the organisation.

There are some important consequences of all this:

- Organisations (and its managers) should be held accountable for the outputs produced.

- Similarly managers should therefore be able to define and guarantee the quality of these outputs, since they have full ownership and control over them

- Managers however cannot be fully accountable for the outcomes achieved – since they do not control them, only influence them.

- The best an organisation can do, usually, is to influence the desired outcome through the quality of the outputs, and investigate the likely and actual relationship between the output and the outcome.

- So start at the back: many organisations are activity focused – ie they are clear about the activities people are spending time on; they have some idea about the outputs these activities are leading to; and often may be quite unclear about possible outcomes.

- If you ask staff what their job is, they will often answer in terms of the activities, rather than the results and the impact they have on the customer (outcome).

- So consider starting from the back: work out what outcomes you want; then think which outputs are most likely to bring those outcomes about; then design/commission the activities that produce those outputs.

OUTCOME	OUTPUT	ACTIVITY

54
ACHIEVING RESULTS:
Sentiment into action

Do you have a vision or value statements, for example:

- · We are customer focused and positive
- · We treat everyone respectfully
- · We are honest and open

Often, these are simply platitudes – statements that can be supported emotionally, and look good on the wall.

For a company to have integrity, to be trusted, and to be credible, it has to put its principles into action; it has to walk the talk.

The best and simplest way of doing this is to ensure that every principle or value is expressed in a range of action statements, linked by one of these three words:

By
Via
Through

For Example:

We are respectful: <u>by</u> listening attentively to others
<u>by</u> being courteous and polite
or

We are positive: <u>via</u> being solution centred
<u>through</u> focusing on what I can do, rather than what I can't do

It's what people do that matters, not what people say.

55
ATTITUDE AND BEHAVIOUR

Your behaviour is a collective term for what you do – how you act; how you show yourself to the outside world

Attitude, is your internal self – the mix of feelings, thoughts, preferences and beliefs that lie (often privately) within you.

Our behaviour is heavily influenced by our attitude………but it is not causal.

Attitude can (and sometimes must) be separated from behaviour.

For example, a negative attitude can never excuse a negative behaviour; people are paid to deliver appropriate behaviours – not appropriate attitudes.

Teachers are unlikely to have a positive attitude to every student they teach; but they must nonetheless behave with that student in a professional way, without prejudice.

As a manager, you will sometimes be faced with someone who either avoids or de-prioritises a task, or does it poorly, because they don't like it, don't value it, or simply don't want to do it. But if it is a legitimate part of their job role, they should do it, and to the best of their ability, despite their attitude.

Given that attitude is such a predictor of behaviour, it is worth trying to influence that attitude; but ultimately, you may have to accept a negative attitude, and still insist on appropriate behaviour (eg introducing change successfully, or addressing racism or sexism).

Imagine how they would feel if you failed to do your legitimate best for them, because you didn't like them, or didn't want to...

One final point: in any 'managing poor performance' situation, you cannot cite 'a bad attitude' as evidence of poor performance – because, since it is internal and private, it cannot be evidenced – it can only be inferred. All evidence must be behavioural. The same applies to 'personality clashes'; the 'clash', to mean anything, must be evidenced; and to be evidenced, it must be behavioural.

56
MANAGING TASKS: 5 Steps

If, as manager, you need someone in your team to do a task – especially if it's new, challenging or complex – you could go through these 5 steps:

1. Clarify the task requirements
2. Check and match to available resources
3. Communicate the above (briefing)
4. Monitor the task
5. Review the task

Clarify the task: this is really all about creating a specification or brief; think through what is required, what key steps need to be taken; what the standards, targets and constraints are; who to involve and consult; what policies or regulations need to be followed; reporting relationships (between you and them); any budget or deadline.

Check and match resources: firstly, identify the resources required; then ensure that resources will be sufficient; if not, obtain more, or change the specification

Communicate: ensure the individual doing the task is clear; give them time to absorb the information; reflect on it; and come back with further questions or ideas

Monitor: On tap or on top?

On tap: available if they need you – so no news is good news, you will assume all is going well unless they tell you otherwise

On top: a supervision (= overseeing) role; invigilation – checking up and progress chasing

Generally speaking the 'on tap' model is more trusting and more efficient – but only if the individual has a clear specification to work to, and will come to you if there's a problem . 'On top' not only has the potential to interrupt and irritate the individual, but takes you away from other jobs you could be getting on with

What ever you choose, say hello and offer encouragement and praise.

Review: signing off the task. What was the result, was it satisfactory? Did they achieve what they set out to achieve? What went well, and why? What went less well, and why? How can that be improved for next time?

Think carefully about the management style you want to use in the above. Generally speaking, there are 3 dominant styles that any manager might use at any time:

- Directive
- Collaborative
- Empowering

Each of the 5 stages can be managed using any of these 3 styles. For example:

Directive: the manager would work out the specification themselves, and the resource requirements, then tell the staff member or team through briefing what was required; they would then supervise, and lead the review

Collaborative: the manager would call a meeting with those doing the task, and though discussion, agree the specification and resource requirements, which someone would write up and copy to the rest. There would be regular meetings to monitor progress, and a final meeting to review the task

Empowering: the manager would give a broad 'headline' for the task, and then ask the individual or team to go away and work out their specification, resources and plan, to present back to the manager who would typically then 'sign it off'. The manager would be 'on tap', and have clarified that no news is good news, and require exception reporting only. The manager would then expect the individual or team to lead a review

All the above can work; all things being equal (!), the empowering style is the most efficient, since it gives a busy manager the most free time to get on with other things....

57
MANAGING TASKS:
The Panto Horse

Proactive—Reactive

The 5 key steps mentioned in the previous section can be allocated into two groups:

Front end: steps 1, 2, and 3   **Back end:** steps 4 and 5

The **front end** steps are where the planning takes place; they are the proactive elements.

The **back end** steps are where the doing takes place: they are more likely to be the reactive steps.

As with any pantomime horse, someone has to be at the front, and someone has to be at the back: both are necessary. Similarly, a manager, in managing a task, will need to be both proactive and reactive.

However, most managers have a preference: they tend to prefer the front end or the back end ....in other words, a tendency to be proactive or reactive.

In the 5-step task management model, a proactive manager will spend a lot of time on steps 1 to 3, because they believe it pays dividends later down the line, particularly for step 4.

A reactive manager will spend little, or even no, time on the first 3 steps. Instead, they will want to get straight on with step 4, and work it out as they go along.

Which part of the horse are you?

The ideal is to be a full horse – to be competent as a proactive and reactive manager, and not dismiss the value of each half….

58
MANAGING TASKS:
Monitoring and reviewing

There is a difference between monitoring and reviewing.

We monitor to control and adjust; it happens live, during the task. Review happens at the end of the task, and its purpose is to learn.

Generally, most managers are more effective at monitoring than reviewing – and there are some obvious reasons why:

- review happens at the end, when the pressure is on to move on: the task is finished, and there's plenty more waiting in the in-tray

- people are tired at the end – they don't want to spend additional effort on an extra task

- if the task has gone well, people would rather celebrate than review; if the task has gone badly, then emotionally the last thing people want to do is spend even more time picking over the bones

- for many, the review stage isn't even thought about – the task is finished....when the task is finished

However, no organisation can call itself a learning organisation if it has no process for learning, and capturing that learning. Review is a very important part of that learning process. So to be more effective as a learning organisation, and to review, here are some ideas:

- ensure review is built into every significant task, and every project

- make the review activity pleasurable

- give people some time between task completion and review – partly so they are less tired, and partly so the review is less emotional, more thought through
- ask people to do a review note, or contribute to a shared learning folder on the intranet – accessible to all
- have someone on the project or task be responsible for debriefing
- have someone on the project or task responsible for capturing the learning that occurs along the way – or ask everyone to keep a learning log or file or diary
- pass on the baton of learning – ensure someone from the outgoing project is available to brief the incoming project team on the learning gained from the first project

59
DEFINING PERFORMANCE:
Time for a glass of PIMST!

If you really want to get to grips with performance, you need to address four issues:

PI   performance indicators

M   measures

S   standards

T   targets

- ie PIMST

Performance indicators: those aspects, characteristics or factors of any product or service that have to be right in order to satisfy the customer. For example, if you were running a teaching or learning session, what would the students want from it for it to be successful (interesting, engaging, relevant, easy to understand...) – ie these are the areas that indicate where the service or product has to perform – ie performance indicators

Measures: you need to know how you are going to measure each indicator. For example, in buying a car, you might be interested in the PI of fuel economy. The measure for this would be mpg (or miles per litre). Many measures are self evident, and a common one is 'customer satisfaction' – ie do they like it (enough) or not? Sometimes different measures produce different results. Using the car example again, how would you measure reliability? Cost of repairs? % of time off road? Number of breakdowns? Each might produce a different result.

Standards: to satisfy the customer, there not only needs to be the right mix of PIs, but each has to achieve a certain level before it can be accepted. So if 'fuel economy' is the PI, and is measured through mpg, the standard might be '40' – in other words, the car has to produce 40 mpg in order to satisfy the customer. So a standard is the minimum level required in order for the customer to be happy.

Targets: whereas a standard is an expectation, a target is an aspiration; it is something to aim for, and ideal. So if 40 mpg is the standard acceptable, the target might be 50 mpg.

As a manager, you need to consider setting PIMST (or the elements that are appropriate) for your staff – or working with them to get them to set them for themselves. You also need to set them for yourself.

PI: Measure: Standard: Target:

Using PIMST:

- helps you think through, in a structured way, what you want from any task or project
- clarifies your expectations
- encourages you to put yourself in the customers' shoes – what do they want?
- makes it more likely the task will be delivered to appropriate and meaningful requirements
- makes it easier for staff to manage their own performance – both by being involved in setting PIMST for their job, but also in using PIMST to monitor and evaluate their work
- it is difficult to evaluate anyone's work fairly if there is no clear yardstick to measure against

- if you are unhappy with someone's work, and you say so, they are likely to ask 'what did you want instead?' (and the inference is – "why didn't you make that clear at the outset?!")

Only use those elements of PIMST that are appropriate and work. For example, not every job will need standards, or targets – it is often one or the other.

60
DEFINING QUALITY –
Wanting the best!

Compare a paper cup and a crystal glass. Get them in front of you.

Which is the quality product?

The answer is, they both are – if they were meant to be like that. They both serve and meet different needs. The paper cup is not a failed crystal glass: the crystal glass is not a failed paper cup. Presumably they have both been designed and built to meet their separate purposes.

So quality resides in the specification, or brief, for the product or service. It is this that sets out the components (PIs) and standards (levels) required. So long as the product meets those requirements and standards, then it can claim to be 'quality'. Both containers are quality products, if they both meet their (different) specifications.

Three interesting conclusions follow from this:

· it is difficult to claim quality in any product or service if there is no specification for that product or service

· whoever owns the specification controls quality

· some products or services can be over-produced as well as under-produced. A Rolls Royce is not a quality product if it was meant to be (and had the budget only to be) a mini….

Often 'excellence' is thought to be the best job possible – in fact, in the real world, excellence is usually 'doing the best job possible with the resources available' (see notes on time management for more on this)

61
DELEGATION:
What it is, and what it isn't

It is:

- vertical – from manager to one of his or her staff
- voluntary – should not be imposed (that is extending the job via the back door, and it will be resented)
- finite – it should return to the manager after an agreed period
- representative of the manager's grade
- supported – not imposed then abandoned

It isn't:

- **dumping**: sometimes delegation is used to offload unpopular, boring or difficult tasks. This does nothing for the person receiving the task (the delegatee) except add to their workload, and lead them to feel exploited

- **work allocation**: many managers misuse the word delegation, when they really mean allocation. Typically as a manager, you will receive tasks which you then need to allocate to the rest of your staff. Assume you are Grade 2 and they are Grade 1. If a Grade 1 task comes in to you, which the staff are paid to do (and you are not), then giving that job to a Grade 1 team member is work allocation, not work delegation. And – if you use the word delegation for this, you might be making a rod for your own back, since the word 'delegation' implies the task originally belongs to you...

- **team work**: every now and then the team will face a crisis, when it's all hands to the pump. In such circumstances, you might call on the team to help you out. That is just good team work (so long as it doesn't happen all the time). You are not really delegating or allocating, you are sharing...

- **time management**: some managers are encouraged in textbooks to use delegation to save time. But not only can this appear as dumping (see above), but if done under time pressure, it is likely to be done badly: no time to brief properly, or supervise, or coach

It is, or should be:

- **developmental**: the person receiving the task should get a benefit from the additional work they are being asked to do. Therefore

    - give the staff member a choice from a list of possible tasks (you control the list, remember)

    - ensure there is something of value or benefit in the task for them – usually something developmental

Good delegation should feel like 'acting up under supervision': it is doing a higher-grade job, but with that person available for support, coaching and advice.

62
DELEGATION:
Why, who, what, how, when

- **why:** to create a win-win-win:
    o the individual wins, because they get the development opportunity
    o the manager wins, both by having developed staff, and by then freeing themselves to get on with other things, while the staff member does the delegated task
    o the organisation wins, by having good cover if the manager is away for any time, or leaves
- **who**: the delegatee should essentially be a volunteer, who sees a benefit in the deal; it should be equal opportunity – not a way of developing favourites
- **what**: the job should always be representative of the grade held by the delegator – the manager. That's what makes it developmental
- **how**: you might like to introduce a formal scheme of development by delegation:

For example
    o explain the principles and processes to all staff
    o ask if they'd like to be included or not (people can join or drop out at any time)
    o then, for those who are in, delegate some of your key tasks to them each on a rotational basis – so if there are 3 staff in the scheme, for example, each gets to do one of 3 delegated tasks on a monthly basis:

	Jan	Feb	March
Person 1	A	B	C
Person 2	B	C	A
Person 3	C	A	B

everyone gets equal opportunity, and no one has the task for life; you get 3 occasions over three months when, in return for one coaching session, you get three sets of free time (and developed staff)

- **when**: on a regular and rotational basis, to suit you and the team.

63
MANAGING OVERLOAD:
Stop whining & decide

Demand and supply
I bet most people including you can feel overloaded, and it's assumed that's because there is an excess of demand (your to do list) over supply (time resources you have available). That is there's more to do than the resources to do them with:

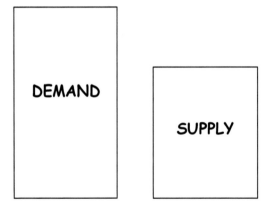

Though each day may start like this, it never ends like this: it is always in balance – demand and supply are levelled off against each other. It's true!

This because either some things on the demand side won't get done, and/or the supply side will have been stretched to meet the demand.

Often this is an accident – but it a good manager will decide whether:

- the demand must be met, and you need to find the resources to do it (demand led management), or
- the demand has to be capped because resources are limited and fixed (supply led management)
- or a mix of both

Here are some suggestions for reducing demand and increasing supply:

Demand management:

- prioritise, and work down the list until out of time/ resource
- (re) educate the customer to limit their demand
- renegotiate a lower specification
- just say no
- redistribute – outsource, delegate...
- let it go...accept some things will not get done
- don't be a perfectionist – work to the standards required, not your own

Supply management:

- be more efficient
- reduce waste
- substitute a lower cost resource
- increase supply (borrow, share, ask for help....)
- increase capacity through training and development
- stretch the supply – usually by giving your own time free

64
POOR PERFORMANCE:
Just tackle it!

AUCCC

Think of someone who is, has been, or might be, a poor performer (it could include yourself...). Make some notes about the examples you have of this .... and then work through this model from top to bottom.

A: Awareness:

- is the person aware of the problem, that there is a problem?· if not, or if you are not sure, make them aware; talk to them

  It is always amazing how many managers just feel too uncomfortable letting staff know there is a problem

U: Understanding:

- find out if they understand the importance or significance of the problem (ie its impact or consequence for the business/service/themselves or colleagues)
- do they understand their own contribution to the problem – what they are doing, or not doing?
- if not, or you are unsure – talk to them; clarify and explain; produce the evidence

C: Capability:

- are they able to do the job? Do they have the skills, knowledge and experience?
- if not, provide the necessary information, training and development

C: Capacity:

- have they resources to do the job – including sufficient time?
- If not, either provide them, or prioritise the person's tasks, or reset the specification so it better matches the resources available

C: Commitment:

- are they motivated? Do they have the right attitude?
- If not, talk to them about this; discover why, and use some of the motivational strategies in this book to help turn this around

Benefits:

Too often managers who see poor performance see it as a commitment issue, when it is often to do with the other four factors.

In fact, if the other four factors are not in place, it is little wonder that the individual isn't committed

Working with your member of staff from top to bottom, through AUCCC will help tackle the easiest problems first: it's relatively easy to make someone aware, and to create understanding. Each factor thereafter becomes a bit more challenging.

The model helps you focus on the issue, rather than the person – ie it isn't Alan – it's their lack of awareness, skill, etc.

It's a structure to help you think logically and constructively through the problem.

65
MANAGING POOR PERFORMANCE:
RKSA

This model is similar to AUCCC, and it is likely you would use one or the other, but not both. Like AUCCC, it's main purpose is to help you **think** through the problem, and it has the same benefits.

Performance gap: the first step is to establish that there is a performance gap (PG). This usually means under-performance, but it could occasionally mean over performance (ie someone is working so hard in one area it compromises their performance in another). To establish this gap, you need to clarify two 'lines': the line of what is required, and the line of what is actually happening – this will produce evidence of the gap. If you cannot provide evidence of a gap, then you cannot really tackle the issue: you must have the evidence

In RKSA: there could be any one or more of four reasons why there is a lack of performance:

R: resources – insufficient resources (including lack of time)

K: knowledge – they don't know what, and/or they don't know why

S: skill – they can't do it, or to the standard required

A: attitude – they cannot be bothered, or refuse

These factors act on each other: if RKS are poor, then A is likely to be poor, too.

Performance can be evidenced only through behaviour. See the section on attitude and behaviour to understand their relationship and importance.

RKSA have a sting in the tail. If poor performance is down to a failure in any of these factors, and you as the manager are primarily responsible for any of those factors being in place – then the poor performer is in many ways, you!

66
POOR PERFORMANCE:
Now for the chat..

SCOPE

Once you have good evidence of poor performance, a meeting is required, but what and how the say it?. SCOPE provides a 5-step structure to build the discussion around. It moves you from problem to solution; from general to specific; from past to present to future; and is a really effective collaborative tool. It will get you both talking and working on the problem, not a telling off!

The 5 steps are:

S: symptom

C: causes

O: options

P: preference

E: execute action

Start by asking how the employee feels things are going; they may well start to identify the problem themselves.

Symptom: then be clear about what the problem is and focus on two things in particular:

· the evidence to show that there's a problem and that something undesirable is happening; clarify any negative consequences

· the evidence to show that the individual is a key factor in that – is to some degree responsible

Cause: Ask what they think is causing the problem – the situation or set of circumstances, the behaviours, that are leading to the problem; get them to talk about what happens – to explain; avoid if you can "why?" – it sounds accusatory and makes it feel like an interrogation (so they are more likely to become defensive)

Options: Even if you don't agree on all the detail, but can agree there is a problem, invite options for improving things. Brainstorm ideas between you, and then discuss the pros and cons of each option

Preference: Try to discover and agree on the option that works best for you both. That way, you are both likely to make it happen; it is less effective forcing your preference on them; they are likely to find reasons why it didn't work. Seek progress rather than perfection; give yourself a time limit for option generation, then choose the one that takes you furthest to where you want to go

Execute action: Once you have made your decision, create an action plan to make it happen – what, who, when. Make your own contribution clear, and also discuss and agree what is likely to happen if this doesn't work – ie there is no improvement

67
MEETINGS:
Make them work ..

Checklist for success

Fed up with ineffective meetings? The checklist overleaf has 33 items that help create a successful meeting. Choose a meeting you normally attend which you dread. Now tick each item that consistently applies or is present in that meeting. Then total the number of ticks.

Scores:

25-33	likely to be effective
15-25	likely to be moderate or patchy
Less than 15	likely to be ineffective

1   the beginning of an agenda is prepared prior to the meeting

2   members of the meeting have an opportunity to contribute to the agenda

3   advance notice of more than 1 week is given of the time and place of the meeting

4   agenda and other useful information is sent to members at least 48 hours prior to the meeting

5   meeting facilities are comfortable

6   the meeting begins on time

7   there is an indication on the agenda of the time estimated for each item

8   each agenda item has more detail than just the title/ heading for that item

9   everyone has a clear opportunity to present their point of view

10   all participants pay active attention to whoever is speaking

11   the chair summarises/recaps regularly

12   no-one tends to dominate the discussion

13   there is a clear note taker

14   there is a clear and effective time keeper

15   all decisions are summarised, clarified, agreed and recorded

16   individuals can be relied upon to carry out their agreements and responsibilities between meetings

17   the appropriate people can be relied on to attend the meeting

18   those attending have the appropriate authority to make decisions

19   those attending the meeting are involved (ie interested in or contributing to) more items than not

20   meetings are not interrupted

21 members stay focused on the agenda topic: there are no side conversations, or wandering off into irrelevancies

22 there is a sense of achievement at the end of the meeting

23 'Any Other Business' is checked (then scheduled) at the meeting—or there is no 'AOB'

24 there are agreed and explicit 'ground rules' (standing orders) for the meeting

25 everyone is clear why they are at the meeting

26 contributions are relevant and succinct: there is little or no waffling or trivialising

27 everyone is clear about the purpose of the meeting

28 meetings do not over-run – there is a finishing time which is adhered to

29 everyone is clear about their own role in the meeting – ie why they are attending, and what they are expected to contribute

30 everyone has prepared appropriately for the meeting

31 members of the meeting behave positively towards each other: there are no personal attacks, put downs or belittling behaviours

32 an action plan (not just 'minutes') are circulated within 48 hours of the end of the meeting

33 the meeting focuses on issues, not personalities

Overall score: _____
How many of the following did you tick?

10	26
12	30
16	31
21	33

There are 2 key factors affecting meeting success: procedures, and behaviours. The 8 numbers above all relate to behaviours. Often these are hardest to control, and have the most impact.

68
MEETING SKILLS:
The role of the Chair

Decide firstly, whether as Chair, you are in a leadership role or a facilitation role (captain or referee):

leader (captain): as this kind of Chair, you are leading the meeting; you are likely to speak first on each item, and have prepared what you want to say. You feel your job is to influence the meeting, and lead it to your conclusions. You want the meeting to support you and your ideas/proposals. Most of your contributions are to persuade, sell, influence, and gain support

facilitator (referee): your role here is to manage process, rather than content; to manage how the meeting develops, rather than contribute to the debate itself. Ideally, as facilitator, you won't have a particular view or concern about the pros and cons of each item: your job is to ensure the meeting runs smoothly. Like a referee, you should manage the game, keep the score, and keep an eye on foul play. You record any goals (decisions), keep time, and ensure rules are followed. You don't care which side wins, and you don't get involved in the game as a player. And, just like good referees, a good facilitator is hardly noticed....

Managing the meeting: whether leader or facilitator, it is important that the meeting has some kind of structure.

There should be an agenda, and each item should have the relevant detail:

· purpose of the item
· outcome required

- background information
- (possibly) time allowed for the item

In managing each item, it might be helpful to use this structure:

- Clarify
- Discuss
- Decide
- Action

Clarify: ensure everyone understands the purpose of the item, the outcomes wanted, and the role they are expected to play ("why am I here?"). It may be important to clarify whether the item is for information, for discussion, or for decision.

Discuss: this is the debate on the item. You either lead on this (as leader) or invite contributions (as facilitator). If the debate is extensive and wide ranging, you should summarise from time to time. Ideally there is a separate note taker who will record the main points being made.

Decide: move the meeting (if appropriate) from discussion to decision. Summarise the main points, and the options available. Decide on the decision making mechanism – consensus, vote, etc

Act: ensure the decision is recorded, and from that, prepare an action plan – otherwise the meeting will have made a decision, which is good, but no one will take ownership of the actions necessary to make the decision happen. So a simple action plan is what needs to be done, by whom, and by when.

69
MEETINGS:
Managing the behaviour

If it is a regular meeting, it is worth investing in a Code of Conduct for the meeting (see 'Team Building: Code of Conduct'). If this can be discussed and agreed by the meeting membership, then:

  · members are more aware of the 'rules'

  · they are likely to own them, having been involved in discussing and agreeing them

  · the Code of Conduct gives authority to the Chair who can refer to it when intervening

  · a statement at the bottom of the Code will really help:

  "The Chair can intervene to clarify the code"

An effective Code, which deals with key procedures and behaviours required, will go a long way to solving most problems. Even so, there will be times when the meeting becomes ineffective – usually due to inappropriate behaviours, such as mini-meetings, waffle, irrelevance, interruptions, belittling or put down behaviours, getting heated.....

Here are some strategies to help you manage the above, as Chair:

  • sometimes it is best to address these difficulties outside the meeting – beforehand (if you know such a behaviour is likely); afterwards, in a private 1-1 (see giving and receiving feedback notes elsewhere). You could call a break, and speak to those concerned in private

- minimise the meeting being dominated by some individuals and introduce smaller discussion groups. So if there is a meeting of 18, and it is being dominated by 2 individuals, you could split the meeting into discussion groups, to report back. Put the two dominant individuals in the same group!

- putting people into smaller groups can address another concern – people who often have good ideas, but stay quiet – either because they are intimidated by dominant members, or because they lack confidence in speaking up in larger, more formal meetings. It is a truth that more people speak if they are put into smaller groups. So creating small groups encourages participation. This allows everyone to contribute and so feel more valued. In forming the groups, it can be useful to put quiet people together; they will talk....

If you feel you have to intervene in the meeting, and particularly on an issue that might seem personal, then the following process may help:

- Think first, before acting: what's the problem? Why is it a problem? What can I suggest to move it on? What words will I use (write them down if it helps). Breathe, stay calm

- Wait for a suitable moment – usually a pause for breath..

- Intervene softly: if appropriate use their name, and ask a softening question: "Derek, can I just ask a question/offer a suggestion/come in here?" (asking a question in this way has two benefits: it is seeking permission to intervene, rather than demanding to intervene; and it gets people listening).

- Acknowledge their contribution: this also acts as a softener; it is courteous and valuing. For example: "what you've said makes a lot of sense/you've made a good point.."

- Then give a reason for your intervention, that is logical and difficult to argue with, and is not a criticism of that individual: eg "Geoff and Susan have both signalled they'd like to come in with a response, and I'm keen to hear their views"
- Then announce what you want to happen: "So can I take a response from Geoff, then Sue, and take it from there?"
- Then seek the approval of the meeting, by looking round the room – not at the individual – and saying: "is that OK?". Generally, if you feel the need to intervene, it's likely you will have the general support of the meeting – they will have been feeling what you have been feeling. Looking around the members and checking; "OK?" brings them into the game, and gets their quick endorsement (usually nodding)
- Say "thanks" – then move on: "Geoff – over to you"

70
PROJECT MANAGEMENT:
A low tech approach to project planning

If large and complex project management is a major part of your job, you may find it helpful to learn some of the high-tech and specialist approaches to project management – eg PRINCE.

If however you have occasional and small scale projects to manage, either on your own or in a team, then this low tech device is a little bit of magic...

- You'll need a set of post its in a range of colours, and a sticking surface – either a wall, or a run of clear tables.

- Then brainstorm all the activities that need to happen from the start to the end of the project – put each idea on a separate post it; you don't need to think of them in order just write down what you think

- Now lay them out in a logical order.

Look for tasks that are logically dependent (you can only do B after A) and tasks that are independent (you could do C and D at the same time if you have resources). These are called independent tasks; the resources must be available for both to happen concurrently.

Where there is a logic dependency tasks, line the post it's horizontally, left to right; independent tasks can be lined vertically.

- Put a time line at the top of the post its so that the horizontal line is matched to a suitable time period (days, weeks, months). Then re-organise the post its to fit this line. (You can if you prefer set your time line first, then allocate your post its, horizontally and vertically, within this time line). It's useful to have a different colour for this time line.
- As you are doing this, new activities will occur – just create a new post it for each activity, and put it in its logical place

When you feel you have finished, put some data on each post it, usually as follows:

- Middle: name of activity
- Top right corner: number of activity in the sequence (doesn't matter if numbers get out of sequence, so long as each activity has a unique number)
- Top left hand corner: person responsible for making this activity happen
- Bottom left hand corner: start date (estimated)
- Centre, under the title: duration (how long in real time it will take someone to complete this task)
- Bottom right hand corner: end date (estimated)

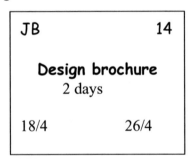

- The gap between the start and end date can be longer than the duration. This is because you can plan for an event to take place in a calendar period longer than the duration. For example, an activity can take 2 days of someone's time – but you might allow a fortnight of calendar time for it to happen.

- To capture this information:
  o Photograph it, and print the photo, using your mobile
  o Copy it directly onto a laptop/PC – and possibly into a computer based specialist project software programme – or if not, onto a spreadsheet...
  o Sellotape across the post its, to keep them in sequence (if you are using a wall for this, it may be best to put flip chart paper on the wall first, so the sellotape attaches to that, rather than the wall...!).
  o Lift them off the surface, collect them together, and then take them away (they can be recreated later if the numbering is sensible)

Major benefits of this approach
  o people find it easier to follow
  o they get involved
  o it's tactile
  o gets people out of their seats
  o teams have more ownership and understanding

71
PROJECT MANAGEMENT:
Hints and tips

- have a clear project specification (see 'Managing Tasks: 5 key steps' – step 1)

- decide on the status of the project team. Is it an operational team – ie the team that will, together, complete the task? Or is it a steering team – ie one that will steer and oversee the project, but most of the tasks will be done by others outside this team? An operational team tends to be larger than a management team, and needs a different skill mix

- be clear about the following key roles, and the relationship between them:

- commissioner (the person or group that called the project into life, and usually owns the funding for the project)

- project manager (the person responsible for the operational management and delivery of the project, and for running the project team)

- project team (whether operational or steering, their roles and responsibilities need to be clarified)

- external support/contractors (people – often specialists - who need to contribute to the project team, but are not full members of it)

- customers/end users (those who are intended to benefit from the project, and who should therefore be consulted at the outset, and throughout the project)

- try to ensure there is no confusion between meeting the needs of the commissioner and the customer/ end user. Meeting both sets of needs, harmoniously, is a key role of the project manager

- have a clear project plan; ensure all key stakeholders are involved in the initial plan, and have a copy once it is finalised; ensure the plan is regularly updated. Have a plan that breaks the large project into bite size chunks, so it is more manageable and less overwhelming; create milestones, key points within the plan which should be reached by a certain date (base camps on the way up Everest...)

- clarify key reporting relationships – how the project's progress will be tracked, and who needs to be kept informed or consulted – how and how often. Consider using exception reporting – ie only reporting the exceptions to the plan, rather than the full detail every time

- agree at the outset a protocol for snags management – especially if the project will cross other departmental or divisional boundaries. In such cases, it is often tricky to get the necessary support for the project from others who are not direct beneficiaries of the project. A useful protocol is shown below:

- under this procedure, the snag would attempt to be solved firstly at the operational level (A & B); if this fails, A will report action taken to date, and lack of progress, to their line manager, (D), who will have a word with B's line manager (C). A & B may also be present at that meeting. If C and D cannot resolve it, then it moves finally up one more level, to the cross over point (E) – ie the manager who has overall responsibility within the structure for C and D. E makes the decision, which all accept. Having this procedure beforehand makes it less likely there will be sticking points – because no one really wants this to move upwards to be solved (since that reflects badly on the abilities of A and B)

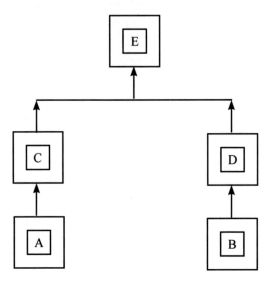

72
PROJECT MANAGEMENT:
The Triangle

Quality

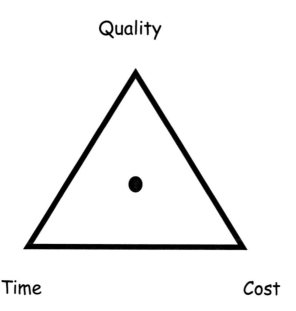

Time   Cost

The black dot in the middle represents your key 'decision point'. At the beginning of any project, you will have it in the middle, equidistant between the three key factors of quality, time and cost: the project always starts with all 3 being equally important. But as the project progresses, the dot will tend to move, and it's important for the project manager and commissioners to decide which 'corner point' is the priority – because (in reality) the more you move towards one of the corners, the more you move away from the other two.

So if quality is crucial, then it may cost more in terms of time or budget to achieve that quality; if getting the project in on deadline is crucial, it may cost more to make that happen, and/or you may have to sacrifice some quality; and finally, if staying within budget is paramount, then the project may be shorter than expected – or sometimes longer – and again, quality might be compromised.

The decision triangle emphasises the need, at critical times, to decide which are your crucial or critical key performance indicators (PIs). If everything runs smoothly, then all PIs can be met, equally; but if they don't, some PIs might actually conflict – maintaining quality standards might simply be costing too much. In such situations, strong management requires the crucial decision: which PI is most crucial?

In terms of running a commercial airline, the three PIs of passenger safety, in flight service and punctuality will all be important. But are they all equally important? If a plane has not enough meals to meet the number of passengers, and it will delay the flight to get the extras needed – what would you do – go on time without enough meals, or sacrifice punctuality to meet the commitment to in-flight customer service? Good management will make the priorities between (potentially) conflicting PIs clear, so that operational staff – lecturers, tutors, learning assistants and administrators make the right decision under pressure.

MANAGING PROBLEMS

73
DECISION MAKING:
Not deciding is a decision!

There's always a choice: you just may not have realised it yet.

The 3 As - Avoid............Act..............Accept

Avoid: one decision is to avoid the issue, pretend it doesn't exist, or that someone else will fix it, or it will sort itself out or go away of its own accord. All these are avoiding the issue. The benefit is that you don't have to deal with it, but the two main costs are that the problem is unlikely to go away, and that you often feel bad about yourself for not tackling it.

Act: address the issue; confront the situation or problem (without being confrontational). The main benefits are that it may solve the problem, and that you often feel better for doing something constructive. The two main costs are that it doesn't improve things – only makes them worse – and the fear that it will not improve things, only make things worse. (Note that it is often the <u>fear</u> of something, rather than the something itself, that stops us acting. So, for example, by fearing the boss will get angry, we never test it out, so we never know if the boss would get angry, and if they did, whether we could handle it).

Accept: it is perfectly reasonable to think before acting, to weigh the pros and cons, and to decide, rationally or otherwise, not to act. If you do that, however, you have chosen to accept. You may not like the idea, but that is what the outcome of avoiding and not acting leave you with.

At this point you have two choices (decisions) to make. To accept positively, or to accept negatively. The former requires you to make the most of the unsatisfactory situation, find the positives in other parts of the job/your life, and decide not to take your unhappiness out on others. Negative acceptance means moaning, grumbling, sulking and generally taking out your frustration on yourself and others

Whatever decision choice you make, you must accept the consequences that come with that choice. You cannot for example choose the (benefits of) avoidance, and not also accept ownership for the (negative) consequences.

74
DECISION MAKING:
Difficult decisions

What makes a difficult decision difficult? The answer lies in the high costs of all the options.

When every option has a high cost attached to it, it is difficult to decide – so we tend to wait, in the hope that a low or no cost option will reveal itself. If so, don't hold your breath. If you've given it time, and all your options are costly, then that is probably the situation that exists. Waiting is postponing. In effect, you are choosing the cost of postponing/avoiding/delay in preference to any of the other options and their costs....

An obvious solution is to look at the costs and benefits of each option, and decide that way. But experience suggests that, psychologically, most people do not score cost and benefit equally. Most people are more averse to costs than they are welcoming of benefits. Put another way, if there is a set of costs and benefits, people tend to focus more on the costs....So the suggestion now is **choose your cost**.

Look at all the options, which all have significant costs. Then choose the cost you can most live with. Recognise that to make any progress, you will need to take a cost along with you – there is no free ride on difficult decisions. So choose which cost you think you will find easier to bear. Then get on with it.

Once you've decided, life becomes easier: you know what your costs are, and you are more likely to invest in the benefits, to help you offset the costs.

75
DECISION MAKING:
Post its and dots

You'll need a few packs of post it notes and some coloured sticky dots.

This is a simple but effective tool that helps in decision making, and has other side benefits too.

It is essentially used to help groups generate options then evaluate them.

The process is simple:

- Announce the problem, or issue, or concern
- Ask everyone to generate as many options as they can, and put them on post its – one page per idea
- Get them to stick their post its on a wall or other clear surface

- Group the post its which are similar, and if there are identical suggestions, leave one and remove the duplicates
- Give everyone some sticky coloured dots. How these are used can vary, but the simplest suggestion is for people to put a dot (any colour) on every idea they support (not necessary to put one on their own ideas)
- You will then have a set of ideas, and a number of supporting dots for each idea – which shows the consensus of support (or otherwise) for each idea
- You can then type up these results, and/or choose the top high scorers and debate them more fully. Or you can simply go ahead with the top scorer as 'the decision'

This process has a number of additional benefits:

- You can collect a lot of ideas and opinions very quickly
- Everyone has equal opportunity – both to suggest ideas and also give an opinion; it's a very egalitarian, democratic process
- This process empowers those with ideas and opinions who are usually quiet, or lack confidence, or who aren't comfortable speaking up in a larger group
- It also neutralises those who tend to dominate group discussions
- People are probably more honest in their opinions (dots). In a normal discussion, people know who has suggested what idea, and may support or otherwise according to source as much as for the idea itself. This process makes it harder to identify whose ideas they are – ideas have an equal status, devoid of source

- It's a very visual process, and very transparent; all ideas and opinions are up for, and open to, inspection; people can see at a glance where the consensus is (and isn't)
- It gets people up and moving about – it's quite energising and social
- You can have several issues on the wall at the same time

Though this has been described under the decision making section, it could equally well be used in the following settings:

- Meetings
- Team building
- Facilitation of away days/strategy sessions
- Business planning
- Consultation exercises (eg focus groups, customer/ staff surveys)

76
DECISION MAKING:
Progress, not perfection

If you check every option against perfection, you will focus on the gaps (since nothing's perfect). As a result, you are more likely to reject each option – which gets you nowhere— and means in effect you are continuing to choose the status quo. Instead, check each option against progress – which option takes you furthest, in cost-effective terms, to where you want to be?

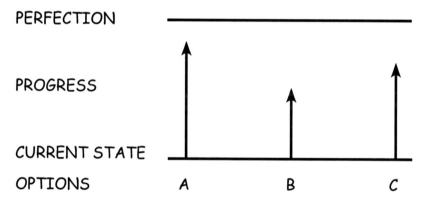

PERFECTION

PROGRESS

CURRENT STATE

OPTIONS   A   B   C

In the above example, there is no perfect option—but option **A** is the most progressive option. So, to prevent delay by seeking perfection, take these three steps:

- set a deadline by which you will stop seeking options
- decide whatever else, to not choose the status quo
- choose the most progressive option.

Once you've done this, you can still continue to seek a better option, but you'll be starting from a better place.

77
DECISION MAKING:
The weighted matrix

criteria

1   2   3

option A

option B

option C

This is an effective decision making tool where:

you have a short list of options

each option has pluses and minuses

you are in danger of going round and round the problem - ie "on the one hand......but on the other hand..."

Key stages

1. construct a matrix or grid - a spreadsheet is ideal
2. set out your options down the left hand side – ie; in the rows
3. set out across the top (in the columns) the criteria against which you will compare each option
4. weight these criteria, by applying a multiplier (x2, x3 etc), according to how important that factor is compared with the others
5. decide your scoring scale (usually 1,2,3)
6. set a quantifiable benchmark value for each score, for each criterion (this is hard, but crucial)

7. score each option against each criterion; each option must score 1, 2 or 3 against each criterion - there can be no blanks

8. apply the weighting

9. total the scores

10. select the highest score option as your decision

11. if your decision doesn't 'feel' right, check:

   are your weightings representative?

   have you left an important criterion off the grid?

78
PROBLEM SOLVING:
Cause, state and effect

Draw a picture of a dripping tap on a blank sheet of paper.

What's the picture?

What's the problem? (Have a go at answering this question before moving on).

If you said:

- · faulty washer
- · not turned on/off enough
- · blockage in the pipes
- · low pressure
- · or similar, you see the problem as cause: ie what is causing the problem.

If you said:

- · it's a tap, and it's dripping
- · it's producing a slow succession of drips
- · there's a tap, and water is coming out of it in drips
- . or similar, you see the problem as state: ie what does the problem look like

If you said:

- · it's making a noise
- · it's wasting water
- · it's creating a slippery surface

- it's causing damage or erosion

- or similar, you see the problem as effect: ie the impact or consequence of the dripping tap

In problem solving terms, only one of these is the correct definition: problem as effect. If there is no perceived negative consequence for the individual or group, then there is no problem for that group, and they will fail to take ownership of the problem.

Something only becomes a problem, if we are aware of it, in terms of negative consequences. Some students who are late or poor attenders, know that it is against the rules, but if nothing serious is likely to happen, then for them there is no problem in being late. But if they want to stay on at college, and after a certain level of lateness has been reached they know they will be excluded – then they have a problem.

The teacher has had a problem all along – because they know (in registration and inspection terms) lateness or non-attendance of students will be frowned on. But because the teacher has a problem, it doesn't mean the student has a problem, too.

Definition: a problem is anything that has a negative consequence for that individual or group. No negative consequence: no problem

In order to get people to own a problem, you have to be able to show the negative consequences for them or those they care about.

79
PROBLEM SOLVING:
3 creative approaches

Association/disassociation
Combinations
Reversal

Association: lots of innovative ideas have occurred because someone has seen something in one context, and transferred the idea to a new context. Here are a few examples:

wine press…………………>   ………> printing press

sink water…………………>   ………> 'float glass' technique

grass 'sticky burrs'…>   ………> Velcro

The above were all 'fortunate accidents': if you want a creative tool, take the following steps:

·   have a problem or issue in mind

·   choose an object, at random

·   give yourself 1 minute to write down all the features, impressions etc about that object (texture, history, function, appearance, materials, weight, etc)

·   when you've finished, go through your list, to see if you can usefully associate any of the object words with your problem; do they give you a fresh way of thinking about the problem? Do they give you fresh ideas or insights?

Disassociation, as you might expect, is the opposite of association. Use the same process, but this time find opposites, contrasts or differences.

Combinations: this is the technique of combining two existing components and making a brand new 'third' component. The best example of this is probably the earliest version of Tippex, which was a combination of emulsion paint and nail varnish remover!!

Create (and keep) a random list of objects. Then, from time to time, take one of the words, at random, and test it in combination with the rest (or a sample) of the words on the list. You needn't have a problem in mind – you are just being creative; but if you do have a problem in mind, see if any of the pairings offer an insight into the problem, and how it might be solved.

Reversal: one of the simplest, but one of the best, and most productive of all creative techniques. Simply reverse the norm....examples include:

· assembly lines (take the components to the worker)

· Domino Pizza (take the pizza to the customer)

· The Fosbury Flop – going over....backwards????

To get you started:

if it's internal, how would it be external? (Pompidou Centre, Paris)

if it's external, how would it be internal? (ID chips instead of collars for pets)

if it's below, how would it be above (container ships)

if restricted, how would it be if always available? (cash points)

if it can't be silent, can we make it noisy? (commemorative applause instead of silence at football grounds)

80
PROBLEM SOLVING:
The 'how to' technique

Write down a problem you have, or have had, or might have.

Now write the problem again, as a set of 'how to' statements: i.e.

The problem is....

- How to..............
- How to.........
- How to..........

Do this, before continuing (use separate paper if you want to keep this page clean).

Now, cross out 'how to' on each statement. What are you left with? In most cases you will have a clearer, simpler, more focused action to undertake.

An example: assume the problem is low staff morale. So, using this technique:

The problem is:

- How to find out why morale is low
- How to find a solution that works
- How to check whether it is the same for everyone
- How to improve morale

Which leaves:

- find out why morale is low

  find a solution that works

- check whether it is the same for everyone
- improve morale

The first two help – they lead to helpful and positive actions; but the last two are less helpful. In this case, either discard them, or use them as a new trigger for a set of 'how to' statements:

If the problem is how to improve morale, then:

- How to find out what would work for them
- How to test it first, to see if it works
- How to find out what works elsewhere

This is a good exercise to do as a team – it can reveal the degree of consensus.

Compare your 'how to' statements to your initial description of the problem. Which do you prefer? Why? A quick & simple technique that takes you from the problem to action.

81
PROBLEM SOLVING:
Brainstorming

Doing it right?

You will have heard about brainstorming, and will likely feel you have used it. But there are some misconceptions, and it is worth clearing them up.

Brainstorming is a short activity – usually 5 minutes. This is because the brain storm should be limited to idea generation.

The idea evaluation comes later. (Idea generation is a right brain activity: idea evaluation is a left brain activity; the technique works best when the two activities are kept separate).

There are ground rules for the brainstorm:

Do

1. Keep it short (5 minutes, high energy)

2. Say whatever comes into your head (no private censorship – that's your left brain at work...!)

3. Even if you don't know why the idea is there, say it – that's your right brain, and you should trust it in this exercise (your left brain can try to work it out later)

4. Tough one but..don't comment on other people's ideas – including 'we've already had that' – that's your left brain again!

5. Keep your ideas clear, simple and specific

6. Have some people in the brainstorm that have nothing to do with the problem – they are 'free' thinkers, with no agenda or defensiveness

7. Have someone record all ideas on a flipchart or screen, so everyone can see them

Next ...

Once the brainstorm is over, the evaluation (left brain) can begin:

go through the list of words, and ask the group if anyone wants any of the ideas explained

then ask the group to split the list into 2: carry forward or discard

if someone feels strongly about an idea that they want to retain,but is being nominated for the discard pile, they can have 1 minute to make their case

throw away the discards

prioritise the 'carry forward' list for discussion

discuss – decide

Easy! and pat on the back if you always do it this way!

82
PROBLEM SOLVING:
In here or out there?

Read the following problem, and come up with your solution:

A man takes his son out for a drive in his car. They are involved in a car crash. The father is killed outright and the son is badly injured. He is rushed to hospital. The surgeon comes into the operating theatre, takes one look at the boy and says, 'I can't operate on that boy - he's my son.'

How can that be? Have a go, before reading on.

Answer?

If you've come up with any of the following you are way off the mark:

- Stepfather
- Priest
- Holy father
- A different father
- It's all a dream

The answer is much more simple: the surgeon is his mother.

If you didn't get this, you are probably recoiling in shock at the moment; you KNOW women can be surgeons; you are NOT sexist; you support equal opportunities......so why didn't you get it??

The answer is in conditioning: we are conditioned (consciously and subconsciously) to think of and see the world in a certain way. If you didn't get this, then subconsciously you still 'see' surgeons as men.

So the problem isn't in 'the problem' – there is no problem in the text. The problem is in you. The problem is not external (in the event); it is internal – in the way you see things.

The important message from this example is this: some (many?) problems we face are not external problems at all – yet we keep looking at them as if they are. And unless we look internally, at ourselves, and the way we see things, then the 'problem' will persist.

83
COMMUNICATION:
7 steps for report writing

1: Clarify the brief
- ask, then answer the following questions:
    - o who (audience, readership)
    - o why (purpose, objective)
    - o what (message, not content)
    - o how (style, structure, format)

2: Brainstorm/mind map the issue you want to discuss
- put the report title in the centre of a page
- mind map possible topic areas (headings)
- then key issues within these headings (sub headings)
- on a separate sheet, make a list of all those sub headings you need to do further work on – then do that work

3: Allocate key points/messages to headings
- open up your PC or laptop
- enter the main headings or sub headings
- allocate (as bullet points) the points you want to make under each heading/sub heading

4: Write up, and expand, on points, using plain English
- connect the points made
- be succinct and direct
- elaborate and expand on the points, to make your case
- then 'warm up' the text, to make it reader friendly

5: Arrange text into an appropriate structure
- organise your headings and key points into a logical flow
- ensure there is a beginning, middle, and end
- **beginning** should include some or all of the following:
    o purpose, background, methodology, overview, summary, contents, glossary
- **middle** is where the main case is made
- **end** should include conclusions and recommendations
    o recommendations should be cross-referred to the main text; appendices should be in the order they appear in the main text

6: Consider presentation/layout issues
- make sure the tone/style is appropriate and consistent
- use bold to emphasise key points
- make the layout visually attractive
- make numbers easy to read (graphs? spacing? shading?)
- number the paragraphs, for ease of reference/ discussion

7: Final check for grammar, punctuation, spelling and sensitivities
- get someone else to check: we don't see our own mistakes that easily
- check for sensitivities—e.g. gender free language

84

COMMUNICATION:
Emails out of control

Consider setting up a '**message board**' within your intranet, to send 'for information' messages, so individuals are not swamped by emails and attachments, and ensure colleagues have the responsibility for keeping themselves updated by checking this message board

Use sensible headings; put relevant information in them. e.g.:

what the email is about

date by which you need a response

some importance classification

This then allows the reader to skim through the email headings, without immediately having to open up each email.

Be careful of unhelpful email chains. If you are making a fresh point to a colleague, start a new email with an appropriate heading, rather than just send a reply, which will have the earlier, but inappropriate heading—and will not be easy to find later

Do you constantly check for a new envelope to appear or wait for the ping on your pc, then stop what you are working on to respond? Stop! you're wasting time. You need to; plan 2/3 times each day to look at them—otherwise your day is constantly interrupted by them

85
COMMUNICATION:
A passport to success

When you're in doubt about how to communicate, follow the passport to success:

P

Personal, not impersonal

"I am sorry that...." (personal)

"It is to be regretted that..." (impersonal)

personal is more friendly and direct

impersonal can sound distant, and even defensive (no-one is taking ownership)

A

Use Active, not passive

"The cat sat on the mat" (active)

"The mat was sat on by the cat" (passive)

passive is less direct, less personal, more boring, invented (synthetic—we don't speak using passive) and longer

passive is helpful when you want to emphasise the process, rather than the doer

S

Simple, not complex

one main idea per sentence

KISS a lot when writing: keep it short and simple

make your main point first: then elaborate with examples and evidence

S

Short, not long

words and sentences and paragraphs

"walk" rather than "perambulate"

"about" rather than "approximately"

sentence of no more than 20 words

more people will understand them

more accessible, less excluding/intimidating

less hard work reading

write to express, not to impress

P

Precise, not vague or ambiguous

"general flies back to front" (military commander returns to war zone)

"he put the cat on the chair and it started to shake" (the cat, when placed on the chair, started to shake)

many (more than a few); most (mathematically more than half)

O

One word, not two

avoid nominalisations (yuk!) - turning a verb into a noun and then having to find another verb to support it:

"we came to a decision" (we decided)

"we gathered for a meeting" (we met)

avoid unnecessary reinforcements:

"totally lacking" (lacking?)

"completely unnecessary" (unnecessary?)

R

Redundancies - **information that is unnecessary**

anything that adds content without aiding understanding: we'd be better off without it

"Please find enclosed herewith a cheque for the sum of £10, to cover the period May to September 2009" ("I have enclosed a £10 cheque for May to September 2009")

"I would like to take the opportunity at this moment in time of thanking you for your patience" ("Thank you for your patience")

T

Their needs, not yours – think of the reader!

Content: what do they need to know?

Structure: will they follow this (I know what I'm talking about—will they?)

Style: how do they like/want it? How will this sound to them?

Layout: will they find it easy to read?

There are usually 3 parties involved when writing: the writer; the person asking for the letter or report to be done (the commissioner); and the end user/audience. Make sure you write for the last one, and not the first two….

86
INFORMATION OVERLOAD

This is another 'out there, in here' problem. In today's world, information overload is almost inevitable; you might be able to reduce some of it, but it will still be too much. So really it isn't about the information—it's about how you handle it.

- Learn to speed read—particularly skimming and scanning. This will help you get an overview quickly

- Prioritise: do not read material in the order in which it arrived on your desk

- Sort into appropriate folders—e.g.:
  - For action (must move on it today)
  - Pending (see note below)
  - For information
  - Filing (to be done at set times)
  - Bin

- Pending: if you have a waiting pile on your desk, use this technique and it will be so much easier to stay on top of this pile:

- Put today's date in the top left corner

- Put the date you next need to see this paper in the top right hand corner

- File it into the pile in date order (soonest at the top)

- Then each day, bring today's papers from the top of the file into your action folder (you can do it again, if it's still not a priority for today—i.e. give it another date..)

- This way the papers will work their way to the top, in date order...

- Always read to a purpose; that way you'll stay focused and concentrate more easily (especially if the content or presentation is boring). As you prepare to read, think: What do I want to get from this? Why am I reading this? Look for key messages and implications

- If you've read something and want to return to action it later, make notes on the paper, or separately but attached, so that when you return to it, you have your first notes available; otherwise, you'll have to start again

- Be clear in both giving and receiving messages. In particular, challenge 'urgent' and 'asap'. What do they mean? If it's urgent, then the deadline must be imminent, so ask for it. Similarly, don't use urgent and asap yourself

- Don't be driven by incoming information—you should manage it, not let it manage you. Set up systems and have personal discipline to do this—e.g.:

- In trays not on your desk, so you are not physically interrupted

- Make it clear to your team when you can be interrupted or not (see tip 88 on interruptions)

- Ask to be taken off distribution lists which you don't need to be on

- Get rid of stuff you know you are not going to use

- Don't keep/file stuff that is already held elsewhere on the system

87
MANAGING TIME:
Deadlines and Durations

The two are not the same!!

A deadline is the date by which the task has to be completed. A duration is the amount of time spent (or to be spent) on the task.

If I asked you to let me have a report in two week's time, how long do you think you have to do the report?

The answer is not 'two weeks': the deadline is two weeks from now, but how long you have to do the report has not been specified. Either it is up to you (depending on what else you have to get on with during the next 2 weeks), or up to me to specify. Notice the difference in this request:

Can I have that report in two week's time—and don't spend any more than 6 hours on it

Durations are important for several reasons:

- It's the duration, rather than the deadline, that controls quality. Two people could each produce the report required in two weeks, but one has spent 6 hours on it, and one has spent 6 minutes. Other things being equal (including effort and talent), the 6 hour report is likely to be the better quality product. Quality is in the duration, not the deadline

- In some jobs, if there are no clear durations (time spends) allocated, it is difficult to control workload. For example, assume a productive 30 hour week. Suppose you had 6 tasks given to you by your manager. Unless you have some idea of how long each will take, then you cannot schedule or plan your week; you cannot give and meet deadlines with any confidence; and you have no idea if the week will be sufficient time to get them all done. (This is true also of your daily plan....)

- Durations are particularly crucial if the job is to be charged on to someone else. Suppose you were asked by a customer to produce a particular service, and you know that the unit hourly cost of producing your service is £50. Assume you have agreed to do the job for that customer for £500. Assuming no profit, just break even, how long have you assumed the job will take? 10 hours (500/50). Suppose the person you have given the job to does not know that—because you haven't given a duration, and as a result (because they are very conscientious) take 20 hours. What kind of a business are you running? One which will become bankrupt.

- Notice in this example too, that if the job is actually higher quality than expected by the customer (because of the extra hours spent), then although the customer will be delighted, they will expect the same service standards next time....

88

MANAGING TIME:
Of course you can manage interruptions

- this sounds crazy at first, but is actually very important. Do you typically get interrupted each day? Does this usually take up your time—both in being interrupted, and in generating extra work that you didn't have planned? Do you make any allowance for this on your daily plan or 'to do' list? If not, you are spending time you have not 'budgeted for'. So:

- work out your typical 'interruption spend' (monitor over a typical fortnight) let's say an average of 2 hours per day

- allow for that figure to be part of your daily 'time spend' - have it as a standing item on your daily plan or 'to do' list, so if you work a 7 hour day only plan to get through 5 hours worth of work

- not doing this explains why often you feel you haven't got done what you planned to have done, and why you get frustrated with interruptions. You'll find that once you make an allowance for them, your daily plan is more realistic, you get more done, and you feel more in control and relaxed

- **planning for interruptions is not the same as scheduling them**—for most people, interruptions come at random and unpredictable times (see tip 88). So the idea of planning for interruptions is the idea of making an allowance for them—accounting for them—rather than saying: 'they can only happen between 10.30 and 11.15....'

- how many of the interruptions you get are a core part of your job—they are why you are there—to answer queries from staff, manager and colleagues. The trouble is, we associate interruptions with bad news—as if they are something to be avoided. This isn't the case. So separate in your mind 'service enquiries' and 'disruptions'; you need to minimise the latter, and manage the former. Stop using the word 'interruption': choose 'service enquiries' and 'disruptions' instead

- you can try to manage your service enquiries better. If you have an open door policy, then great—but don't grumble about being 'constantly interrupted'! Encourage staff to make appointments, or let them know you have set times each day when it's OK to interrupt. Use your door as a valve—open means 'come in'; closed means 'can it wait?'

- distinguish with your staff a 3 level process for managing information:
    o Interrupt: if they need to see and discuss, now
    o Appointment: if they need to see and discuss, but not now
    o Note: if then need to see, but not discuss, and not now

- remember, staff and colleagues are not mind readers; if you have a preference, let them know. Establish a preferred pattern or routine, then let people know; then thank them when they fit in with it.

89
MANAGING TIME:
Sort your priorities

Most managers realise that it is important to sort their workload into priorities, then work to get through as many priorities as possible.

How do you decide what is a priority?

These are legitimate factors for deciding:

by importance: yes—but how do you decide what is important?

The following all work for us:

by 'added value': which tasks contribute most to your team, your organisation, the customer (you may get different answers depending on which of the above is a priority!)

by risk: which tasks will produce the biggest cost if they go wrong?

by dependence: if I don't do this, other people will be held up and waiting further in the line—i.e. they are dependent on this task

by fret factor: if I don't do this, I will just worry about it, and that stops me being effective—so best to get it done and out of the way

Avoid prioritising using these factors:

by sequence: by order in which they arrived at your desk

by source: i.e. who has asked for this task to be done; though it is tempting to use this to prioritise, the main reason should be importance, not source (easier to say than do, though...)

by urgency: again, be careful (see tip 92 on urgency...)

by personal preference: do most what you like- MOST DO THIS

But....what if everything's a priority?

In other words, you've got rid of your non-priorities and low-priorities, but you still have too much to do, and they are—all—priorities....!

There are two solutions to this: scheduling and discipline.

Scheduling

Each day, the aim is to get through as many of your priorities as possible. The temptation is to start with your most important priority and work on down, through the list, through the day. But imagine your top priority is to finish writing a report; your second, third and fourth priorities are to read and sign off on a 4 page note, and make two phone calls (in that priority order). Suppose too that the beginning of your day is very busy, but you usually are quieter over lunch, and after 4 pm. Then it might be sensible to make the quick phone calls (priority 3 and 4) first thing, because they can be quick, and it isn't easy to be disrupted when on the phone, then do the other two priorities at your known quieter times (even going somewhere quiet). The principle here is—select from your priority list in a sequence that suits the pattern of your day.

Discipline

Give yourself a duration and a deadline for each task, and stick to it.

90
MANAGING TIME:
Opportunity cost

An opportunity cost is the opportunity you give up of doing something, by doing something else. Simply, by doing task A, you cannot at the same time be doing task B. So by doing task A, task B will have to wait, or not get done at all.

Reading this, now, is task A. You are therefore giving up the opportunity of doing something else instead (task B). So reading this had better be worth it…!!

And that's the point: when trying to decide what to spend your time on, from all the competing demands, use the idea of opportunity cost to help you decide.

Simply: is what I'm about to spend my time on worth more than anything else I could be spending that same time on? If not, why am I doing this, and not that?

So the opportunity cost of staying late chatting is not taking the kids to the park….

The opportunity cost of dealing with something urgent may be not doing something important… (see tip 92 on urgent v important)

91
MANAGING TIME:
Time budgets

This relates to the section on durations.

A time budget is an allocation of time spend for any particular task. Having a time budget:

- allows the manager and the individual to have a better sense of what's expected, in terms of both the time spend, and the quality required

- helps the manager and the individual 'block out' the workload in a more realistic way. Without this it's possible to allocate a list of tasks, with deadlines, which is completely unrealistic

- acts as a control for the individual—i.e. gives them something else to work within other than the deadline

- time budgets can only be estimates—and as such, they are guesswork. But once they have been given, the individual and the manager can tell whether the task is over-running, under-running, or 'on schedule' - so it's then easier to make adjustments

- we do this all the time out of work: for example, if flying abroad for a holiday, you'd estimate how long for the journey to the airport, and for checking in, etc—so why not do the same at work?

- if the task is huge and complex, break it down into bite size logical chunks, and put an estimate against each of them—and so build up the overall estimate

92
MANAGING TIME:
Urgent and important

Urgent and important are not the same.

Most people prioritise by urgent. But if you do, this is what happens:

- everything becomes urgent. Everything you do has become urgent—that is why you are doing it. So prioritising by urgent becomes a self-fulfilling prophesy. As a result:

- you are always working under the pressure of urgent; this can have its benefits, particularly if you genuinely feel you work better that way; but for many, it is stressful, and produces mistakes

- even the important becomes urgent—which may not be a great idea. Imagine you had a report to submit that would decide whether your unit was disbanded or not—an important report. But it isn't needed until 3 months time. Do you need to do it now? (no). Is there something more urgent needs doing today (yes). Then the important report is postponed, and postponed—until it becomes urgent. But, given its importance, it would probably have been a good idea to begin earlier, to allow plenty of thinking, consultation and reflection time. So some important happens too late:

  - getting a tooth seen to when it's too late
  - paying attention to your spouse when...
  - giving up smoking when....

- some important never happen at all—because it never becomes urgent:
    - watching your kids grow up
    - taking that trip...
    - telling someone you loved them...

Set out below three things in your life that are important to you:

1

2

3

Ours might be: it is important to be

1 happy

2 loving

3 healthy

Now try the same exercise using 'urgent' instead of 'important':

It is urgent to be:

1 happy

2 loving

3 healthy

It doesn't work; it's a different vocabulary.

It's as if there are two conveyor belts in life: one is the belt marked 'urgent' and the other marked 'important'. By travelling on the urgent belt, it is difficult to get onto the important one...!

Suggestions:

- ensure your 'to do' list includes a mix of urgent and important—and keep both moving
- if a job is important, but not urgent, and its importance means you shouldn't leave it to the last minute, then put a 'start' date in your diary—and stick to it.
- urgent deadlines are usually finish dates
- important deadlines are usually start dates
- take a look forward to look back: in 3, 5 or 10 years time, what do you want to have done? What will matter to you then? Make a list, and pin it somewhere visible, every day.
- make sure it happens proactively—otherwise it won't happen reactively. Have you ever intended to go to a film, play or concert—but missed out because you didn't book your ticket? Make sure you book your tickets for the important things in your life
- **NEVER blame lack of time**: we all have the same amount—it's what we do with it that counts. Take responsibility for your time spend—and don't hide behind 'I didn't have the time' - how come other people mange it then? Blaming time is an excuse, and one which actually stops you achieving—because, if you think it's a time problem, you are waiting for 'it' to improve (don't hold your breath..!)

93
MONEY: It isn't a resource

This seems a crazy thing to say.

However, money ISN'T a resource: it's simply the most convenient, available, acceptable and flexible way of acquiring a resource.

A resource is what you actually NEED to do the task. Money is the usual/normal way of getting that resource.

To get from Manchester to Edinburgh you may need transport, fuel, tickets, a route, and so on. These are resources. But you could get them by other means...

Many managers concentrate on money as a resource, rather than on the resources themselves. Consider other (legitimate) ways in which resources could be acquired:

Exchange

Gift

Loan

Substitution

Sharing

Invention

If managers sought to use more of the above as alternative 'acquisition routes', they would a) not be so dependent on money, and b) would have more of that commodity (money) left for those things that only money can buy....

94
SYSTEMS & PROCEDURES:
Business planning

Business or service plans come in a wide range of forms, and use a number of different ways of producing them.

Some thoughts for you:

- have a clear specification for the plan: who is it for; why are we doing it; what does it need to say; how do we prepare and present it?

- start at the back: what outcomes do you want? What are the success criteria for the plan?

- following on, you may want different versions, with different (levels of) content, for different audiences

- think of who you want to involve, and how. This should be influenced by who you want to use it. People have more ownership of it if they are closely involved in its construction. So if you want operational staff to use it, then involve them in the process: involve, not inform (e.g. away days, focus groups, surveys....)

- will there be a 'nest' of plans—i.e. corporate, faculty, school, team, individual? If so:

- how do they connect/cross reference?

- is the process essentially top down, bottom up or both?

- how do a nest of vertical plans link and cross reference to other plans elsewhere (i.e. horizontally)?

- in covering all the above, does the process and documentation become too unwieldy?

Suggestions:

Many of these suggestions depend on the answers to the questions on the previous page. However:

- make the plan use-ful: then people will contribute to it and use it. If it is only going to end up in a filing cabinet, they won't
- where you can, incorporate other planning processes into this plan—i.e. once only handling; why have separate processes, each with their own documentation, timescale and drivers, when one could do the lot. So consider if the following can all be incorporated in the BP and its process:
  - Direction (vision, mission, drivers and strategy)
  - Operational plans
  - Resources (inc budgets)
  - Performance management
  - Staff development (including appraisal/PRD)
  - Staff welfare—including reward and recognition
  - Internal/external links
- involve people to create ownership, and make the involvement fun (day out; active—for example, using post its and dots)
- use simple forms and language that people can relate to
- above all, make the plan a means to an end, not an end in itself

95
SYSTEMS & PROCEDURES:
Performance review & development (PRD)

All organisations have PR&D in some form or other (sometimes still called 'Appraisal'). It is clearly an important tool, and done well, is very helpful to the organisation, manager and individual. But often it is regarded with cynicism and scepticism.

Here are some suggestions to avoid the main difficulties.

- make sure it is a means to an end, and not an end in itself. This requires two things:
  - a clear purpose: what is it for? What are its outcomes meant to be?
  - clear and beneficial results: What happens to the key documents once they have been completed? Does anything happen? Are staff told/kept informed? Do things change/ improve? Are my training and development needs responded to?
- ensure the documents support the process, instead of being the process. If both manager and staff see the meeting(s) as 'we need to fill in these forms', then that will be the purpose, and is unlikely to excite either of them. Suggestions here include:
  - have no documents, or open documents; instead, explain to both parties what they should cover and record, then leave it up to them how they do it
  - have the conversation, and only complete the documentation after the conversation

- o make the documents simple, clear, and limited in number
- one size may not fit all; you can have standard outcomes without standard processes and documentation.
- some staff complain of 'poor' management of the process by the line manger. **If this is you**, get the following things right (your staff will be looking to you particularly for these):
- set up and run the whole process sensibly and sensitively, taking staff needs into account (e.g. notice of meeting, preparation)
- meet your commitments, to show you take it seriously (if you don't, why should they?). For example:
  - don't cancel the meeting
  - see everyone
  - treat everyone equally
  - follow up on commitments made
- no surprises: PR&D should be tied as closely to operational management as possible. So if there's a need or opportunity for feedback to staff—give it there and then; don't save it
- do what you can to meet their needs within your remit—don't just rely on HR; can you offer development through arranging coaching, shadowing, delegation and mentoring?
- get away from the formulaic approach—e.g. 1 big appraisal and 2/3 intervening progress reviews; instead, run monthly 'light touch' meetings (10-15 minutes), which review performance and development, and provide a simple record. This way, there can be no surprises, and staff will know, from these sessions, what the outcome of the 'set piece' session will be

96
CHANGE:
12 key steps to making it through..

1. Define the change required
2. Identify and sell the benefits (& costs of not changing)
3. Assess and build support
4. Assess and build resources
5. Plan the change
6. Consult and communicate
7. Clarify key roles, including your own
8. Launch the change
9. Implement the change
10. Embed the change
11. Evaluate the change
12. Learn from the process

General hints and tips

Step 1: summarise the change—and its purpose—in a simple sentence; explain what will change, why, and how; use the KILN technique (point 98)

Step 2: show a direct link between the change and the benefit—i.e. "this change....will produce this benefit..."; if a top down change, and you don't know, then find out from your manager; review/explain costs of not changing, too

Step 3: who are your allies? who is likely to be resistant? who is undeclared, or you don't know? have strategies to tackle all 3 groups—keeping allies on board, and using their support; overcoming resistance; finding out about the others, and getting their buy in

Step 4: do a resource analysis: what resources do I need; how vital are they? how easy are they to get? how do I get them?

Step 5: the plan is the means to the end; the route, rather than the destination; this should include launch, implementation and embedding stages

Step 6: think of the 3 I's—inform, involve and inspire. Remember though that turkeys don't vote for Christmas: you cannot let the consultation process be used to frustrate actions you are committed to. So be clear, in any consultation process, what is negotiable and what isn't

Step 7: who is going to do what? what is your role and commitment? Where there is resistance, emphasise the need to be professional; we may not like it, but it's part of our job to do it....

Step 8: a launch gives focus and impetus; it also commits you to action, and to success; it allows you to create and use symbols to associate with the change (colours, logo, launch publicity....)

Step 9: simple action planning: what, who, when. Establish key milestones

Step 10: making the change is easier than embedding the change; think about driving a car. For most people, they 'learned' how to do it quite quickly; they 'knew' how to accelerate, brake, change gear, etc. But it took much, much longer for the ability to drive to become embedded—i.e. automatic, unconscious. Many change strategies focus on making the change—not on embedding the change—yet that is often where the difficulties lie, especially if you are trying to change habits, attitudes and behaviours

Step 11: this is easier if you have clear outcomes/success criteria at the outset, and are monitoring against them all the way through

Step 12: this contributes to being a learning organisation— the need to sign off through 'what have we learned' - so this can be captured, recorded, and passed on or into a central file, for others to use

97
CHANGE: Comfort zone challenge

Most of us live and work in 'comfort zones'; they are different for each of us, and of course vary (and hopefully extend) throughout our lives.

By definition, a comfort zone is comfortable - it's where we like to be. We are confident and happy there. Equally, by definition, anything outside the zone is uncomfortable.

Change often threatens the comfort zone. It takes people outside the zone, creating discomfort, uncertainty and even threat.

However, the only way of ever extending the comfort zone is to move beyond the existing zone—into an area of discomfort. Almost all progress has to begin with discomfort. Think about some of the following that you are now comfortable with:

Driving

Riding a bike

Swimming

Getting (and staying) fit

Playing a musical instrument

Holding a live frog, spider, snake or rat

Giving a talk/presentation

Giving difficult feedback

Doing your current job

Of course, some of the items on the list may still be outside your comfort zone. Some of these may not matter. You may struggle to hold one of the animals listed, but unless you are a vet or work in a zoo—it doesn't matter. You can stay in your comfort zone, and leave these animals alone.

However, there may be items on the list, and other items not on the list, where you are equally uncomfortable, but cannot afford to let them be: either because they are negatively affecting your life; or because they are part of your job role (e.g. giving presentations, giving difficult feedback). In the work case, you are not doing your job properly if, due to discomfort, you avoid doing them, or learning how to do them well (i.e. staying in the comfort zone).

For you, and sometimes for your staff, they need to change. And this means coming out of the comfort zone. As a manager you need to recognise when you need to do this for yourself; and for your staff, you need to understand their fears and discomforts, and offer training, time and support.

Remember: in order to be a good manager, sometimes you will need to be comfortable with discomfort.

98
CHANGE:
KILN

KEEP:	IMPROVE:
LESSEN: (REDUCE, REMOVE)	**NEW:**

This is a useful tool to help you (and your team) take stock. It's quick, productive and fun to do.

Give everyone post its.

Ask them to write down on a post it, everything they would like to keep about the team, the section, the job, the environment—anything that affects them at work

Then do the same with the other three, in sequence: what would they like to increase or improve? What would they like to see less of, or decrease, or be removed altogether? And what would they like to see brought in that would be new (perhaps they've seen it elsewhere and thought 'why don't we do that?', or 'wouldn't it be great if we...')

Ask them to put their post its on a clear surface (wall or table). Then ask them to read other people's suggestions, and either tick or initial them, if they agree (or you could use sticky dots....). You can then collect these in and collate them, and feed back the results. You will have lots of ideas, and a clear consensus on which have team support, and which do not.

This is a great starting point for change, for two reasons.

Firstly, the model itself is pro-change. Only one of the four boxes offers 'no change' - i.e. 'keep'. The other three, whatever the suggestion, is pro-change. So it is a model that, quite quietly, gets people committed to change.

Secondly, wherever there is a strong consensus for change, you have an opportunity for a quick win—because staff will be behind the change.

You can add one refinement to the model, either during or after the process. You can ask people, when they suggest their idea, to nominate a score of 1, 2 or 3 against each idea. The numbers represent ownership: 1 means we all need to do this; 2 means the manager needs to do this; and 3 means its down to someone else outside the team to make this change happen...

99
CHANGE:
Ladder of participation

This is worth using as a checklist when involved in the consultation stage of change. The four rungs of the ladder (starting at the bottom) are:

<u>in partnership</u>
<u>involved</u>
<u>informed</u>
<u>in the dark</u>

You should decide the level (or rung) of participation you want. Keeping staff in the dark is not really an option; it is counter-productive and unethical: people have a right to know. The only exception would be if you have been told something in confidence. Keeping people informed keeps them in the loop, but is one-directional; giving them genuine involvement is likely to create better understanding and ownership. Partnership is the highest form of participation, when staff are, and are seen as, equal partners.

100
CONTEXT:
Climate control

In any meeting which you are responsible for running, there is always a prevailing climate, which helps set and maintain the mood. Usually this climate is neglected or mismanaged. It's your job as a manager to identify the climate, and if negative or restrictive, try to move it to something more constructive.

Consider the two lists on the next page.

The left hand list is likely to set a negative mood or climate, one in which it would be difficult to make easy progress. The list on the right, however, would produce a much healthier climate in which to conduct business.

What could you do to move any of these factors from left to right—literally, to create the 'right' climate?

This is another example of 'positive intervention' mentioned elsewhere: the need for a manager to intervene if it isn't going well. Managing the climate might be a subtle and effective contribution—especially if those involved aren't doing it intentionally—it's a blind spot.

FROM:	TO:
Problem	Solution
Past shaping present	Future shaping present
What we can't do	What we can do
Set to disagree	Set to agree
Negative body language	Positive body language
Negative tone/words	Positive tone/words
Destructive contributions	Constructive contributions
Blocking/rejecting ideas	Building on ideas
Taking separate positions	Looking for shared interests

We hope this book has been useful. If you would like information on other titles or other recommended reading visit our website at

www.effective-training-development.co.uk

Lightning Source UK Ltd.
Milton Keynes UK
UKOW051106030112

184670UK00003B/1/P